So Your Son Wants to Play in the NHL?

Dan Bylsma & Jay M. Bylsma

M&S

Canadian Cataloguing in Publication Data

Bylsma, Dan, 1970-
    So your son wants to play in the NHL?

ISBN 0-7710-1793-6

1. Bylsma, Dan, 1970-   . 2. Hockey players – United States – Biography.   I. Bylsma, Jay M. II. Title.

GV848.5.B95A3 1999   796.962'092   C98-932916-X

Originally published in the United States by Sleeping Bear Press.

Printed and bound in the United States.

McClelland & Stewart Inc.
The Canadian Publishers
481 University Avenue
Toronto, Ontario
M5G 2E9

1 2 3 4 5   03 02 01 00 99

To the memory of our darling little baby daughter and granddaughter
January 15, 1998

"You lit the Paschal Candle before we got to know you."

The preparation *is* for life.

CONTENTS

"This is the best hockey advice since 'Don't rile Gordie Howe!'"

—JAY GREENBERG, Columnist *New York Post* and *The Hockey News*

I

EARLY YEARS

JAY

I remember sitting just behind the players' bench in the Molson Centre, the huge new arena where the Montreal Canadiens Hockey Club of the National Hockey League play their home games. The Los Angeles Kings were skating through a pregame practice. I was watching the player in the blue practice jersey with Number 42 on the back of his helmet. This player was my son, Dan Bylsma. This was the first time I had seen him in an NHL practice. That night for the first time I would be present to see him play in an NHL uniform. That night he would play in the Mecca of hockey—the home arena of the Montreal Canadiens. I was so filled with emotion, I had to fight back tears and draw my breath through a very tight throat.

I never intended for him to play in the NHL. I never planned, never wished, never thought—I never allowed myself to dream he would play in the NHL. This may be one of the critical reasons why he made it to the NHL. Because it wasn't my plan, my wish, my thought, my dream. It was his. I now know *his* dreams began when he was very young. And preparing him for what he was to become began even before that, on June 25, 1963.

That was another time in my life when I had to fight back tears and struggle to breathe. I was standing in front of a window in the corridor of Blodgett Memorial Hospital in Grand Rapids, Michigan, watching a nurse clean up a squirming little newborn baby, Scott Alan Bylsma, our firstborn and Dan's oldest brother. There was no way anyone could have prepared me for what I felt. There was the expected relief that he appeared to be normal and healthy. There was expected joy in the miracle of this little creation. There was the expected feeling of love toward and union with my wife with whom I had made this child. There was also the very unexpected feeling that my life was no longer my own. I belonged to this little guy. I remember saying words to him, words heard only by him and me, "You've got a long way to go, little guy, and I will be there every step of the way."

I've had the opportunity to repeat those words to four more wee entrants into our growing family. It's occurred to me since that I never once thought to say, "I know how to help you every step of the way." I had a Master's Degree in Business Administration from the University of Michigan, one of the finest universities in the world. Nancy, my wife, was a Registered Nurse. Between us we had nine years of post-high school education and not one class in child rearing, arguably the most difficult and important job we would undertake. It struck me recently, that when you go to the store to buy a VCR, it comes with a thirty-page manual in three languages. We went to the hospital to have a baby and we got a handshake and a wish for luck.

With no manual, we used the tools that were apparent and available. We were a two parent family, one of whom was home all the time to tend the nest and fledglings. We used the church as a point of reference, a moral compass, to provide answers to life's most difficult questions. We used the Christian day school where we knew the education would be good and the children would be instructed with an emphasis on the moral traditions in which Nancy and I were raised. We used the dinner table as a place to roost once a day, catch up with each other, and give daily tutoring in our version of Psychology 101. And we used sports as a means of allowing the children to venture out and learn about life in a controlled, wholesome environment.

So the preparation for parenting Dan started with Scott. It was tuned with our second, Greg, and honed with Jon, our third. It was not dreamed that it could possibly become a preparation for the NHL. It was thought to be a preparation for life as most average people know it. Preparation to enjoy its opportunities and bounties, to handle its disappointments, to be a contributing member of society, to " . . . brighten the corner where you are," to confront the ultimate realities of life with a measure of confidence.

It began and it continued with "being there." Being there to be the ones who were the nurturers, the disciplinarians, the encouragers, the teachers, the trainers, the role models, the coaches, the photographers, the fans. And by the time Dan was born, there were five of us nurturing, disciplining, encouraging, teaching, training, and serving as role models. The poor kid never had a chance to be anything other than patterned after the collective five of us.

There was nothing unusual to notice when Danny was born. We had just moved our family of three boys to Grand Haven, Michigan, a small town on the shores of Lake Michigan about forty miles west of Grand Rapids, Michigan, to a four bedroom house with a flat backyard. Four bedrooms because we were expecting this fourth child; a flat backyard because we had begun building ice surfaces each winter in our small backyard in Grand Rapids.

We began to build ice surfaces after Nancy had purchased a small pair of double runner ice skates for our oldest son, Scott, for his fourth Christmas. A few days after the holidays, she announced that her father had always built an ice surface in their backyard when she was a youngster. The implication was that if I aspired to be a good father to my children like her father was to her, I would become an ice surface builder.

I aspired. The first surface was all of fifteen square feet. Scott used to get bundled up and go out and scratch around with his little hockey stick and puck. One day that winter we drove past a city-built outdoor ice surface and saw a number of kids skating about as if they had wings on their feet. I called the boys' attention to the skaters. "Look at those kids flying around that big rink."

After a moment of silence Scott said, "Daddy, would you please buy me a pair of easy ice skates like those kids have?"

We found a small pair of hockey skates in a few days. After realizing that they were anything but "easy ice skates," Scott got the hang of it and was soon buzzing around our little surface banging pucks off the railroad ties that bounded our yard and his little ice world.

The next year the surface was expanded to twenty-by-forty-feet. Number two son, Greg, had graduated into the small pair of single runner skates. Scott had persuaded him to be a goalie and soon the neighbor boys discovered our rink and the shinny games commenced.

The next year we flooded our L-shaped backyard: twenty-by-forty-by-twenty-feet. Fortunately, it didn't seem to matter to anyone that the surface was irregularly shaped and that the goalie at one end had to peer around the edge of the garage in order to watch the action at the other end.

A job change took me to Grand Haven and after commuting for a while, we set about finding a house. The criteria was simple—a flat backyard and four bedrooms because Dan was on the way. I found a backyard that was perfect. We would be able to have a ninety-by-thirty-foot ice surface and it came with a house with four bedrooms. It also came with great next-door neighbors—the Bakers.

Their two small boys (about the same ages as our oldest two) came up the hill that separated their house from the one I was looking to buy. "You got any boys?" one of them asked me. Two little burr-heads looking for playmates.

"I have three boys and maybe a fourth one on the way," I said.

"We're gonna have a baby, too," the boy said brightly. "Your boys play sports?"

The burr-heads, Mike and Ed, and their entire family were to become good friends of ours. The boys would join in the endless games of hockey and baseball in the flat backyard.

There was nothing spectacular about Danny's birth. Nancy and

I didn't feel he was a particularly large baby. Our next-door neighbor, however, Margaret Baker—a Registered Nurse like Nancy—remarked once that he was built well. "It looks like this one might be a football player," she said. Our pediatrician at the time also told us that Dan had exceptionally broad shoulders and "a good solid build."

The environment into which Dan was born and grew up was characterized by love and by competition. Unconditional love and in-your-face competition. In the spring and summer, it consisted of endless games of work-up (baseball) in the flat backyard with imaginary men on second and third base and their current baseball heroes being imitated in pitching and batting. When the ability to hit the ball outgrew the boundaries of the yard, the ball was changed in composition and size and the bats became skinnier until we were down to plastic golf balls and broom handles.

In the fall it was pass-and-tap football. I was the "all-time quarterback," and to get a "first down" you had to advance the ball past the middle sprinkler head in our yard. We endlessly executed the pick-pick-pass play and four-steps-down-then-cut-over-the-middle pass routes.

In the winter, the ice surface usually was put down between Christmas and New Year's Day. If the weather cooperated, we could play our shinny games until the middle of February. I didn't realize when I bought the house that the septic system was located under the flat backyard. While Erma Bombeck's axiom "the grass is always greener over the septic tank" is true, Jay Bylsma's corollary is equally true: an ice surface built over a septic tank will melt from the bottom up. The heat from the warm water being expelled into the tank rises and melts the surface from the bottom up, causing a pocket under the ice. There is a hollow sound akin to thunder when you skate over this pocket. It also is the spot that melts first in the fading days of winter, and sometimes you have to skate around the area over the septic tank.

As the years went by, the ice rinks and the hockey played on it began to get serious. We got a snowblower to help clear the surface and to make side boards out of the snow that fell. We put up a wire fence to prevent errant pucks from disappearing into the drifts in the neighbors' yards. A neighbor whose kids skated with us made proper size frames for goal nets out of stainless steel bars. With some old tennis nets laced together, we were almost regulation.

At first, we kept an empty mayonnaise jar just outside the back door for toilet emergencies. It's another Bylsma corollary that the younger you are, the sooner after you get into your hockey equipment you will have to use the toilet. Later, we put an addition on the house and engineered a wooden staircase to the basement where we built our version of a locker room with an official toilet. It was a considerable improvement over the mayonnaise jar.

When the rink was operational, we would suspend bedtimes and all of us played; the kids went out after school and homework, and I joined them after supper and under the lights. When finally we quit, either because I ran out of gas or Mom turned the lights out on us, we sat in the locker room and watched the steam rise from our sweat-soaked jerseys. While our bodies cooled down, there was a quiet time of reflection about the game just played. We rarely talked about who had won or who had scored. We had played hard, we had sweated, we had tried this new maneuver or that and it had worked or it needed work, and we knew sound sleep with dreams of hat tricks scored before frenzied fans would come without effort. We savored these moments, and I relished being a kid again. Spending this kind of time with my children made for defining moments in building our relationships.

Some of my earliest recollections of Dan are of him donning his older brothers' gear and imitating their games. A little tyke in diapers wearing a red helmet, maneuvering a tennis ball through the family room with a sawed-off hockey stick. Or sporting the protective gear of a Little League catcher that would take years for him to grow into. Sometimes, when he would attempt to throw the ball while wearing a too-big-for-him helmeted catcher's mask, the helmet would spin on his head and he would momentarily appear to be playing sideways.

By the time he was five, Dan had joined these endless games of hockey, stickball, football, and golf in the backyard. At first, his brothers indulged him because I had indulged *them* at that age and because it was cute to see the little guy swing the bat or buzz around on that small pair of "easy ice skates." Before long, he was playing because he could compete. He couldn't play at Scott's level but he could play at Jon's. "Fair teams" became Scott (the oldest) and Dan (the youngest) against the middle boys, Greg and Jon.

There were endless games, encouraged by Nancy and me, because we could see the bonding that was occurring. Instinctively, the lesson that was learned was that success comes from preparation and skill comes from hard work. It also kept their minds off girls. You can't get cooties from a hockey stick but you can from girls. Unless, that is, they're your sister. Laurie was born November 7, 1974. I phoned the school to tell Scott that she had arrived. I later learned that he had gone to Greg and Jon's classrooms and told them, "Bad news. It's a girl."

Nancy and I were thrilled to have a daughter, and the boys' disappointment softened when her first gift at the hospital was a kid's hockey stick painted pink with flowers and topped with a pink ribbon. They conceded she might have some redeeming value. Many years later, Laurie's opinion about being the only girl with four older brothers was succinctly expressed when she pointed out that after four tries, her parents finally got it right.

Sundays were special days. We all went to church and attendance was mandatory. (Where else are you going to acquire a moral compass and where else were the ultimate questions of life addressed?) Church would be followed by a big dinner. Then it was off to the nearest ball diamond and we would while away the afternoon in our inter-family competitions. Actually, at first these long afternoons were encouraged by Nancy. She relished our being out of the house and having a few hours to herself.

Once she suggested she would like to come along and play some tennis with me; the kids could "watch and learn." She had been taking beginning tennis lessons with some of her friends. She thought the fun was to see how long you could keep a volley going. (The kids received a lot of wonderful characteristics from Nancy but being competitive wasn't one of them.) As for the kids, they were bored after about fifteen minutes and took to fidgeting along the sidelines and grumbling "This isn't a game!" and "What a joke this is!"

Then Nancy made a big mistake. "Oh, you think this is easy?" she asked. "You think you can do this?"

Eleven year old Greg was all over that challenge. "Mom," he said, "I could beat you and I've never had a racket in my hands before." I explained the rules and showed him how to hold the racket. Nancy thought she would help the boy out by being the first to serve. Unfortunately, it was just about the only time she got her racket on the ball. If she stayed at the baseline after her serve, he would dink the ball just over the net. If she *charged* the net after her serve, he would lob the ball over her head—and always to her less than proficient backhand. For Nancy, the sport was social: a time for fellowship and relaxation and it wasn't polite to deliver an overhand smash or a drop shot that your opponent had to exert himself to return. For Greg, "polite" was behavior required in a restaurant. From her lessons, Nancy knew how to hit the ball. From observing, he knew how to beat her. Greg, as well as the other boys, had learned that every game is as much intellectual as it is physical.

From then on, tennis was added to the list of family sports.

When Scott was ten, he discovered my golf clubs. They had been packed away in the basement, abandoned in favor of coaching Scott's Kids' League baseball team. He and Greg devised a nine-hole course in our backyard. It began at the gas grill, went to the tall oak, then to the telephone pole, across the water (driveway) to the sprinkler head, etc., etc. We went quickly from the nine-hole course in the backyard (which suddenly was being mowed without any parental reminders) to a few sessions at a nearby driving range to, "Dad, will you take us golfing?" I called Crockery Hills Golf Course, a public course located outside Grand Haven, to inquire when I might bring out two small boys to teach them the game without interfering with anyone else. The following Saturday, Scott and Greg (who was eight at the time) and I were standing on the first tee at 6:30 in the morning. After listening to my stern instructions about the protocol and etiquette of golf, we played the first hole. Scott scored an eighteen and Greg a twenty-two. Both of them were ready to quit.

"You may go back to the clubhouse or sit in the car and wait," I told them, "but I paid to play nine holes. I'm staying; I'm playing."

They stayed, too. On the second hole their scores were thirteen and sixteen and it got better from there. At the end of nine holes, it was, "Can we keep playing, Dad? Please, can we? Huh? Can we?"

By the time Dan was five, he and Jon had sets of clubs and my father-in-law, John Oole, the man who had inspired the ice rinks, had joined us. It became a Saturday morning summer ritual. John met us at the course at 6:30. Thanks to the Garzellonis, who owned the course and allowed us to bend the rules, we played a six-some. Between nines, we stopped and had hot dogs with all the fixings out of a wide-mouthed picnic jug in the trunk of Grandpa Oole's car. "Grandpa's Brunch," we called it.

The ninth hole at Crockery Hills has woods on the left and high rough on the right. It also runs parallel with the eleventh. Teeing off on the ninth one morning, Jon hit his drive to the left and Dan hit his to the right. I told Dan, "I think you can find your ball in that rough, so we're going to help Jon look for his in the woods. When you find it, keep playing toward the green."

After searching the woods for a few minutes, I looked across the fairway to check on Danny and saw him standing at the edge of the rough staring at the ground. He was idly swinging his little club like a sickle, and had his back turned to an elderly gentleman from the eleventh hole who was searching the same area. When Dan did not respond to my call, I sensed trouble and trotted over. As I approached, I saw Dan was crying and asked him what was wrong.

"That man has my ball," he said through his tears.

I turned to the man. "Excuse me, sir. Is it possible that you found the youngster's ball?"

"Could be," the man replied. "What was he shooting?"

I asked Danny what ball he was playing but he just sniffled and shrugged his shoulders. Before I could reprimand him for not knowing, a lightbulb lit up in my head and I turned back to the elderly man. "Sir," I said, "would you mind showing my son the ball you found so he can tell if it's his?"

His irritated reply was, "Doesn't he know what ball he's shooting?"

"No," I answered. "He's only five and he doesn't know how to read yet. But I'm sure he'll be able to identify it if you show it to him."

The man's annoyed expression softened as the implication of what I had said sunk in. "Geez, I'm sorry," he said finally. "Is this your ball, young fella?" He held out an old, off-brand golf ball that was clearly much the worse for wear and water hazards.

As Danny nodded, he reached into the pocket of his shorts and pulled out a brand new Maxfli. He held it up to the golfer.

"That's *my* ball! You had *my* ball," the man said. "No wonder I couldn't find it."

"You had *mine*," Danny replied, sniffling. "And you wouldn't give it to me."

That year, and for several thereafter, golf, baseball, and the dinner table were pretty much how life was lived in the summer. Nancy drove the boys to the golf course at 9:00 or 10:00 in the morning with money for pop and candy bars. One of us picked them up in the late afternoon. Chances are, they would have played thirty-six holes or more. After replaying the day's rounds at the dinner table—hole by hole—they were ready for their baseball games in the evening.

In the winter, it was a different story.

By the time Dan was six, the older boys had been playing organized junior hockey for some time at the indoor L.C. Walker Arena in Muskegon, twenty miles to the north of Grand Haven. This was a house league program, which means all the kids who sign up for a specific age group are divided into teams of about fifteen players. A few practices are held and then the teams play one game a week for twenty weeks. It is a league that accepts all players regardless of ability, and they only play games in the rink where the league is formed. Generally speaking, a house league is the lowest level of organized amateur hockey.

A travel team, on the other hand, is formed by holding tryouts to select the best players to represent an area and age group. These teams often practice two times per week and play two or three games weekly for the seven-month season. They travel to rinks in other cities and sometimes even other states and countries.

In our area, there were no travel teams because hockey hadn't yet advanced to that level of sophistication. So the kids played in the house leagues. Occasionally, the director of the league chose the best skaters and took them to play the travel team of another city. It was a good chance for our kids to compete against better players.

One year, the director of the league asked me to coach a collection of kids he had selected from the teams in my son Scott's age group. We held a practice to see who would play on which lines. We borrowed jerseys from one of the teams, and traveled to Grand Rapids to play their travel team—the Grand Rapids Rockets. It was my first exposure to travel hockey. While our kids had different colored socks (some had different colored socks on *each* leg) the Grand Rapids Rockets had matching jerseys (with the player's name lettered on the back), pants, socks, helmets and even matching equipment bags. Rocket parents in the stands (many of them wearing matching jackets) had organized cheers; most of the parents of our players were back home in Muskegon.

As "Here we go Rockets, here we go! (Clap, Clap)" resounded through the arena during the pre-game huddle, I said to our players, "Listen up, you guys. No one ever got beat by matching pants and fancy equipment bags. I watched them warming up, and it's clear to me that some of these players are on this team because their parents can afford the expensive uniforms, not because they're good. I bet they're over in their huddle right now snickering and making fun because our helmets and socks don't match. Let's go out there this afternoon and make sure that's the only fun they have."

The final score was a whole bunch, to not nearly enough, in favor of the team with the mismatched helmets and socks.

Two things struck me about that game. One was the intensity of the Rocket coach and parents before and during the game. The other was the sense I got from them that the loss seemed to have been unfair. Not unfair because we had cheated, but unfair because they had spent more money, the players had practiced more, and they looked better from a team picture standpoint. The team with the mismatched helmets and socks had no right, no business winning that game. A travel team doesn't lose to house league players. It just wasn't right.

There was also a lesson in this experience for the kids. Ability comes from hard work, not fancy uniforms. While clothes may make the man, a uniform does not make a winner.

Since there wasn't a program for kids under nine years of age, and because of our family's successful involvement with the house program, I was able to persuade the director of the league to allow six-year-old Danny to play with the team of nine-year-olds that Jon played on, and I had been assigned to coach. I'm sure I sounded like a hockey father overestimating his son's ability. Fortunately, Jon's team was short a few players. The director, Jim Bird, agreed to let Danny play if he could compete.

I remember Dan's first goal as clearly as I can remember what I was doing when I learned that President Kennedy was shot. He carried the puck in from the left side and shot it as he darted in front of the goalie. He got tripped almost immediately, landed on his back and I can still see the little legs and stick pumping in the air— pure excitement over his first goal in organized hockey. He came back to the bench sporting a pumpkin-like smile, including missing front teeth. I thought he couldn't have been happier if it were his first goal in the National Hockey League.

His first goal in the NHL proved me wrong.

In the spring of 1978, a job promotion led us to move to Orland Park, a suburb on the southwest side of Chicago. I looked at houses and building sites for three months before finding five acres at the edge of a forest preserve. I bought it from a man who was living in Switzerland. I called him on the phone, told him I had this big active family and would like to build a nice home with a big play area in the backyard. I later learned that many people had tried to buy this parcel before he sold it to us. We must have been destined to get it; my religious tradition would say it was God's will.

In addition to being next to the forest preserve, the site that was to become our home was located half a block from Silver Lake Golf Club—a forty-five-hole facility. We learned very quickly that it was owned by the man who lived right next door. Speaking of the will of God . . .

We situated the house in such a way that we could build a 120′ × 70′ ice surface and use that area as the fairway for a seventy-yard golf hole. We used the excess dirt from digging the house's foundation to build up an area for a small green and to make the backyard level. Although it was a lot of effort, it allowed the kids to play in our yard—and the kids still have people coming up to them reminiscing about the grand games that were played there.

We also incorporated a second stairway, in the garage, to the basement. This entrance to the basement opened into a large locker room with a bathroom and a shower. Thinking ahead, and for only ten dollars, we had two putting cups sunk into the floor of the basement when the concrete was poured. By installing outdoor carpeting, we had our own putting green on the floor of the Bylsma locker room.

Because of a building material shortage, we saw that the house wouldn't be ready in time to move the family for the opening of school in the fall. The builder happened to live in the neighborhood and he invited Scott to live with his family until the house was ready. This allowed him to start his freshman year at his new school, something Nancy and I thought was important. So Scott lived with the builder, I lived in a small apartment near my work, and the two of us went home on Friday afternoons to be with our family. Early Monday mornings, we drove back to Chicago.

Thankfully, Scott seemed to adjust well to his new surroundings and new high school. As a freshman, he was one of the top players on the varsity golf team. The high school had no hockey program but we heard of a tryout being held at the Southwest Ice Arena for a Triple A Bantam Team. Scott had no equipment in Illinois but we dropped in anyhow to evaluate the talent. We met the owner of the arena, Mr. Frank D'Cristina. When he learned we were from Michigan and that Scott played hockey, he insisted Scott try out for the team. He rummaged around and found a pair of skates and gloves.

As I watched from the stands, it was clear to me that Scott would be an impact player on this team. D'Cristina obviously agreed. After the tryout, he pulled us aside and told us what a great opportunity this would be for Scott. D'Cristina said his goal was to assemble a team that could win the national championship. He also told us that the coach was former NHL player Lou Angotti, and that the team would be spending Thanksgiving in Pittsburgh and Christmas in Toronto. We were assured that Scott could play a leading role in the team's success.

I must admit that I was intrigued because it was a chance for Scott to play on a world-class team, the kind of opportunity many parents dream of for their children. And it was being handed to him on a platter.

On the way home, I asked him what he thought about playing on D'Cristina's team. Scott didn't hesitate with his answer.

"In the first place," he said, "I'm away from home too much as it is. The thought of spending every weekend on the road and being away for Thanksgiving and Christmas has absolutely no appeal to me. Secondly, there were some irritating little jerks in that locker room who have no idea of how good they *aren't*. It would really take something to tolerate those turkeys for a whole season. So," he said, "if it's all the same to you, I'll pass. I'd just as soon play in Muskegon on the weekends."

It was a time when my principles got pinched for overstepping my own advice. For a fleeting moment, I was tempted to push him in the direction of this opportunity. But then, how much could I ask of him? I had already uprooted him and put him in a new surrounding without the benefit of his family for support. At what price does one try for the brass ring? In the end, Scott made me understand that it wasn't my brass ring, it was his. And his decision was clear: not this ring, not this time.

Not long after the holidays I received a call from the coach of a Single A Bantam team that played out of the Saints/Spectrum Ice Arena in Chicago. He wanted to know if Scott would be interested in playing on the team during their weeknight games. The idea appealed to Scott so he became a weeknight warrior for the Chicago Saints A Bantam Team. He made a significant difference, too. They began winning and eventually qualified for the State of Illinois A Bantam Play Downs. The first game was on a Friday night against a team from Naperville in their home arena.

The Naperville team had whupped the Saints earlier in the season so they probably assumed this second meeting would be another easy victory. Because of successes over other teams, they had visions of state championships dancing under their hockey helmets. It turned out to be a night that Scott and I will never forget, and for a variety of reasons. One of them, unfortunately, was it brought into very sharp focus some of the things that can go wrong with amateur athletics.

Scott scored five goals and the Saints won the game. I watched from the stands and from his first goal on, the rumblings from the Naperville fans grew louder and more ominous. Stuff like: "If that kid's a minor bantam, I'll eat your shirt!" And: "It ain't fair; that kid's a ringer!"

They were talking about my boy.

After the second period was over, it seemed to take *forever* before the teams came back on the ice to finish the game. Angry parents were huddled here and there talking, some in hushed tones and some in loud voices. They were talking about Scott . . . Scott the cheater.

Finally, the teams came out to play the third period. When it was over there was an announcement that the Naperville team had registered a formal protest, accusing the Saints of using an illegal player. We passed through the lobby amidst a lot of angry stares and some not so friendly comments and headed for home.

"What was going on back there?" Scott asked me once we were on the road. "Someone came in our locker room during the second intermission and wouldn't let us back on the ice until we all signed some paper."

"They were not very happy about losing," I said. "They think you're a ringer. They don't believe you're a minor bantam."

"Joke's on them," Scott said, showing some of the maturity he would be able to pass on to his brothers. "The state hockey commission has a copy of my birth certificate. I'm nothing if I'm not a minor bantam."

A while later we learned that the Naperville protest had been upheld. The Saints only had one goalie and the tournament rules required two. To satisfy the rules, the Saints had a goalie from a younger age group dress and sit on the bench to satisfy the requirement for two goalies. The younger goalie did not play, but he was deemed to be an illegal player. On that basis, the protest was upheld.

As I said, it was example of what can go wrong with amateur athletics. It was also another bad taste in my mouth from some of the adults in travel hockey who get too wrapped up in their goals for their children and too wrapped up in their unrealistic expectations.

The finish date for the house was extended all the way to March. It meant the kids had to enter their new school in the middle of the spring term. Nancy and I felt bad about putting the kids through it—new kids on the block *and* in school—but I'm sure their first day was harder on *us*. Spring sports were just beginning and their abilities were welcomed and so were they. Sports had a very big payoff here in an unexpected way. It could have been music or painting or some other skill that gave them confidence, self-respect, and standing with their peers. But for us it was sports.

Our next-door neighbors, the Coghills (owners of the golf course) happened to have girls who were the same age as our children. It wasn't long before their girls were in our swimming pool and our boys were playing golf on their course. Constantly. Occasionally, our two oldest boys were hired to compute blind bogies, Callaway handicaps, and the scramble scores for large outings at the course. A twilight search of the water hazards was usually good for a sack of golf balls, which, after a short cycle in Mom's Maytag, yielded three or four dozen that were good as new, and a lot of clay in our septic tank.

It wasn't long before the boys' golfing abilities caught the attention of Matt Carvey, the teaching professional at the course. Coincidentally, Matt was the supervisor of maintenance and buildings at the Whiting Corporation where I was the Controller. He was close to retirement age and a small, wizened man who could work magic with his golf clubs. The kids took to "Matty" and he to them. He gave them free lessons from time to time and taught them trick shots, like hitting a golf ball with the back of the club head and hitting two balls at once and then catching one of them in your pocket. He also supervised the building of the green in our backyard.

Matt would often hire Dan to collect golf balls after one of his lessons was over and before the next lesson started. Dan would patiently wait in the golf cart while Matt struggled with duffers who had spent a lot of money on lessons and clubs in hopes of improving their game. At the end of such lessons, Matt would say to his pupil, "I want to show you how easy this game is. This is Dan. Dan is eight years old. Dan, hit your driver for this gentleman."

Dan would tee up a ball and hit it about180 yards down the middle of the practice range. Matt would turn to the astonished duffer and say, "See how easy it is. A little kid can do it."

Sometimes Matt would show up at my office at the Whiting Corporation and say, "That little one of yours, don't ever let anyone touch his golf swing. It's a keeper."

When hockey season approached, we investigated available programs. With four boys playing, travel hockey—with its additional cost for ice time and time-consuming trips—was both a financial hardship and a logistic impossibility. Yet the boys were clearly Triple A caliber players. If they didn't play travel hockey, would we be holding them back from fulfilling their potential? The answer came from an unexpected source.

One day, I was listening to a radio talk program on a Chicago station. George "Sparky" Anderson was a guest on the show. He had recently been replaced as manager of the Cincinnati Reds baseball team and was entertaining telephone calls from the audience. One caller's question and Sparky's answer provided a blinding flash of the obvious.

The caller related that her son was a high school baseball

player whose coach had predicted he "couldn't miss" making the major leagues. The coach was pressuring her to send the boy to an expensive baseball camp which the single mother could not afford. With a catch in her voice, she indicated she was willing to beg, borrow, or steal the money as she did not want to stand in the way of the boy making the major leagues. What should she do?

I have repeated Sparky's answer to hundreds of parents in the same quandary. "Madam," Sparky said, "save your money. Your son will make the major leagues *in spite* of what you do for him, not *because* of what you do for him." And if that wisdom was good enough for Sparky Anderson, it was good enough for the Bylsmas.

The Oak Park Ice Arena was not far from where we lived and it appeared to have a house league program suited for all of the boys. When we arrived for registration, I attempted to get Danny (who was now seven but had played the previous season with ten-year-olds) on a team with players of similar ability. The league authorities insisted he play with his age group. One official told me: "If we accommodated every parent who thought his kid was a future NHLer, the league would be a mess. He plays with his age group or he doesn't play."

Scott's, Greg's, and Jon's applications met with the same inflexibility. Danny's team won its first game six to one and it was Danny's first career double hat trick. For the rest of the season ("To make it fair for the kids on the other teams," I was told), Danny was only allowed to play the first two or three minutes of each period. We attributed his ability to the fact that he had already been playing in the backyard for several years and had older brothers to emulate.

More than half of the boys in Danny's league also played on at least one travel team. As was my experience in Grand Rapids, playing on a travel team didn't necessarily equate with talent or skill; it equated with the parents' ability to pay the additional cost and their often unreasonable expectations. Some seven- and eight-year-old youngsters would come into the arena for an early Saturday morning game looking half asleep. They had played a late game in a northern Chicago suburb the night before and would play a third game on the far West Side that afternoon.

The parents of these players repeatedly asked us to consider having the boys play for this or that travel team. In their eyes, it wasn't right for a player as good as Danny to miss the "opportunity" of playing on a travel team. Just think how good he *could* become if he traveled over two hundred and forty miles every weekend to play two or three more games. Because some of these parents were the same ones who complained that he scored too many goals, and had lobbied league officials to limit his play, I was often tempted to ask if he would be allowed to play the whole game if he joined a travel team.

Instead, I implored the league officials to move Danny up to the next level. When they finally agreed, the coaches at the next level wouldn't allow it unless he played on *their* team. They were fully aware that even when he only played the first few minutes of each period he would still score five or six goals a game. From this experience, we learned that travel hockey wasn't the only place to find contemptible behavior. There were adults in house leagues, too.

Scott fared a little better. Playing in the midget division (fourteen and fifteen year-olds), with Greg as the team's goalie, he scored five or six goals a game. He also began to do end-to-end rushes, after getting passes from Greg, so that Greg would get the award for the most assists. It would have been novel for a goalie to win that award, but it was a mockery of the game. Wisely, I thought, Scott was soon moved up to play in the high school division for a crusty, old veteran coach by the name of Mr. Boudreau.

The first time Scott played for him, Mr. Boudreau came into the locker room with his customary pre-game cigarette cupped in his hand. He looked Scott in the eye and said, "You may have been hot stuff in the lower league, kid, but so far you haven't shown me s—." In his own brand of eloquence, it was Boudreau's way of deflating any ego that Scott might have obtained from playing at the previous level. Scott's response was to score three goals and two assists in a winning effort. After the game, Boudreau congratulated him by saying , "One game doesn't mean s— to me, kid."

In spite of Boudreau's gruff demeanor, Scott eventually endeared himself to the old coach. In the last game of the playoffs, Scott scored five goals in a 3-2 victory (two of the goals were disallowed for reasons that were not made clear to Boudreau, but on which he had opinions, verbalized in unforgettable fashion for all to hear anyway).

When Scott was moved up to the high school league, Jon (who was ten at the time and scoring at will in *his* league) was moved up to play with Greg in the fourteen and fifteen year-old league. Because he was given Scott's old jersey to wear, he took a lot of mocking from players on other teams. Comments like: "What's the matter Number Nine? I thought you were supposed to be so good." Number Nine was not out of place but he also wasn't scoring five and six goals a game, either. Appropriately, Greg fell out of the race for the assists trophy.

Our trips to the Oak Park Ice Arena were family affairs that were eagerly anticipated by all of us. After Danny's game was over, the older boys would play and Danny would watch or be stick boy for one of their teams. Each of the boys were frequently invited to play on travel teams and/or in a number of hockey tournaments. For me, the defining moments of the season happened on the ice surface in our backyard. Night after night we neutralized the icy clutches of the Illinois winter and the politics of overzealous parents and coaches by working up a body-drenching sweat in our endless games of shinny and showdown.

Building and maintaining the rink was always a tedious and difficult endeavor. Standing in subzero temperatures for hours, often in shifts through the night, spraying water on the frozen snow while the rest of the family members were snug in front of the fireplace or in warm beds, taught us lessons. We learned that very little in life is free. Working together gets a job done faster, and that one can take pride in doing one's best. In our work and in our play, we defined work ethic. We defined perseverance. We defined belonging. We defined competition. We defined acceptance through effort . . . regardless of age or innate ability.

And for us, it defined family.

About a year after my promotion, the company I worked for merged with a giant conglomerate and my job went from being a financial officer of a New York Stock Exchange-listed company to little more than a plant accountant. When I also learned I didn't like the people I was working for, the daily commute in suburban Chicago traffic suddenly didn't seem worth the aggravation. I quit my job. We moved back to Grand Haven just before school started that September, and I opened a securities broker/dealer firm with an old friend.

We also decided to build a duplicate of the house we had built in Orland Park. Of course, it had a *bigger, flatter* backyard and enough room for our "golf course." We used the excess sand from the foundation to build another golf green, complete with a bunker. The longest hole, if you could hit a low hook through the woods or a power fade over the chimney, was 130 yards. The kids would pretend to play whatever tournament was on TV that weekend.

Since the house wouldn't be ready in time for the start of school, we moved our belongings into the garage and our family of seven into a small rented cottage with two tiny bedrooms.

Scott would be starting his junior year at West Michigan Christian High School. He knew some of the students because many of the kids from his former elementary school fed into this high school. But he was still the new kid on the block. Greg would be going into the ninth grade, Jon the seventh, and Danny the fourth at the elementary school they had left one and a half years earlier.

Scott quickly became the #1 player on the high school golf team. He frequently shot in the 70s and could drive a golf ball—as we liked to describe it—farther than most people drive on vacation. During the rules meeting at one of his first matches, he noticed that the hole diagrams on the score card were not representative of their length so it was difficult to determine the distance from the tees to the hazards. He asked the opposing coach how far it was to the creek on the first hole.

"Don't worry about it," the coach said, "you can't reach it."

"Maybe not," Scott replied. "But I'd still like to know." It was clear that the opposing players wondered who this new guy thought he was. Scott persisted but the coach was adamant that it needn't concern him.

Teeing off in the first group, with the coaches and all the other players watching, Scott hit his drive into the creek . . . on the fly.

There was only an incredulous and embarrassed silence.

Fortunately, the ball in the water did not prevent Scott from winning medalist honors or the team from winning the match. Scott also gained a reputation in his new surroundings. Once again, it was sports that eased the acclimation to a different environment. It happened to our other children as well.

When hockey season began in October, the boys were happy to be back playing in Muskegon Junior Hockey. A new house program had formed, run by a different recreation department, so the kids got to play twice a week in the different leagues. In addition, Tony Chiasson, a doctor from Muskegon, had formed a Junior 'C' team from some of the better seventeen- and eighteen-year-old skaters in the area. Scott was invited to play. Dr. "Tony" was a good person with a highly developed sense of family and sportsmanship. Being from Montreal he knew something about hockey. It was a super experience for Scott and enabled him to play with some of his old teammates. Even more important, the level of hockey was challenging and it enabled him to further develop his skills. The other boys continued to play hockey as well. Jon and Dan were teammates, and Greg played on a team with Ed and Mike Baker, our former neighbors.

As hockey wound down in the spring, baseball started up. Scott tried out for the high school team and came home from the first few practices with high expectations of earning a starting position. However, the school's basketball team had gone to the state finals and many of the players and the coach were also in the baseball program. When the season started, Scott didn't. Game after game he rode the pines. The coach was comfortable with the kids he knew, most of whom were seniors, and he didn't know Scott.

There is little a parent can say sometimes that will fix a tough situation. "Bide your time and be patient," I told Scott, "When you get a chance," I said, "and you *will* get a chance, be ready to make the most of it. Wally Pipp got the flu one day and Lou Gehrig filled in for him. Pipp never played again. Did Gehrig suddenly get good? No. Gehrig got a chance."

Before long, so did Scott.

The team's first baseman, a star basketball player, became ineligible for one of the games and Scott took his place in the lineup. After hitting home runs in successive trips to the plate, he became the team's regular cleanup batter. Did the coach suddenly become Casey Stengel? No. Did Scott suddenly get good? No. Scott simply got a chance and he made the best of it.

From bench rider to hitting cleanup with two swings of the bat. I was proud and happy for him, and pleased for me. Proud and happy that he had hung in there . . . and pleased that my advice had turned out to be right. Failure is the rule for which success is the exception. It was sweet to see exceptional success.

That summer was also Danny's first at playing organized baseball. It meant there would be eight games a week for us. But regardless how hectic the schedule, there was one inflexible rule: the supper table is family time, and everyone will be there. The rule was never difficult to enforce. All of us *wanted* to be there. Nancy was an excellent cook and there was food and fun enough to go around twice. We took turns telling about our day, the events at school, or some competition. Riddles were told. Theology, politics, or the national news of the day were discussed. Scott once opined that he learned as much at the table as he did in Psychology 101 in college.

During Danny's first year in baseball, the endless games of work-up paid off; he proved to be one of the best players in his league. He made the All-Stars and then won the game for his team by hitting a home run in the bottom of the last inning. We attributed his skill level to the very special gifts he had been given.

When school started in the fall, Scott was a senior and Greg was a sophomore. They became the #1 and #2 players on the golf team. Thanks to some surprisingly good scores on a snowy Saturday in late October, the team qualified for the state championships in Class D. Class D is comprised of smaller schools, some private schools, and some schools who recruit students based on athletic and academic achievement.

When the tournament was completed, Scott was tied for medalist with a player from Detroit Country Day. With the entire field and gallery following them, Scott made a par on the first hole of a sudden death playoff and won the state championship.

I was not aware of how much the older boys were listening for Danny's footsteps (sportswise) until I got a report of Scott's phone call home to announce that he was Class D State Champ in golf.

"Hey, Danny! I've given you something to shoot for, pal."

"Did you win it, Scott?"

"Yes, I did."

"Good. I hope to be there someday."

When hockey season started, I became co-coach of the Junior 'C' team that Dr. Tony had previously handled. Jim Federighe, the father of one of the players, Terry, was the other coach. We played junior varsity teams from Ferris State College (now University), the varsity team from Calvin College (a Division III school), some good high school teams from Jackson and Lansing, and other Junior 'C' teams. Most of the kids also played against one another in various house leagues in Muskegon. Greg was our goalie.

Jon and Dan played together and would do so until Jon left for college. After Scott left for college, Jim Federighe (his other son, Tony, was a year older than Danny) and I would form pickup teams for the better kids in Jon's age group and play in tournaments in other cities. Danny and Tony were always included on those teams. This gave the kids valuable experience against quality teams, without the grueling schedule required in most travel hockey programs.

In Danny's house league, he battled to the wire for the scoring title. To win it, he needed at least a hat trick in the last game and for the current leader, a big redheaded kid named Tim Schuppe, to go scoreless. Danny got his three goals, but Shuppe got one as well and took the title. Tim was four years older than Danny.

Two of our players used that Junior 'C' team as a stepping stone to play college hockey. Scott was able to impress Bowling Green State University's highly regarded Division I program and was recruited to go to B.G. for hockey and golf. Terry Federighe used his 'C' experience to secure a commission at the Air Force Academy. I'm not sure if there was any correlation in the fact that the sons of the fathers who were most involved got the scholarships, but I'd like to think there was.

The following spring, I expected Greg to join Scott on the high school baseball team. But Greg was well aware that the coach favored upper classmen and that Scott had ridden the bench for half the previous season. Consequently, there was no way he would be talked into playing baseball. He had been an All-Star every year that he played in the Kids' League program, but he sat out his sophomore and junior year in high school. Unlike his older brother, he wasn't willing to wait for a chance to prove his worth.

Once again, my principles got pinched a bit. I thought Greg would have played a significant role on the team and it would have been fun to watch our oldest boys compete together. But to push him to play would have had him reaching for *my* idea (again) of what the brass ring was. Greg was his own person and would reach for his own rings in his own time.

That summer, we gave Danny permission to enter one of the National Junior golf tournaments. The closest one to Grand Haven was the Little People's Golf Tournament in Quincy, Illinois. We entered him in the ten-year-old group and Nancy, Danny, and I traveled to Quincy to the Cedar Crest Golf Course. When we arrived, we were not prepared for what we encountered.

All over the parking lot were motor homes with the contestants' names lettered on the side. There were quite a few travel vans and trailers. Our Ford station wagon, to say the least, looked a bit out of place among all the Lincolns and Cadillacs. Many of the kids had brought along their own teaching pros, and a lot of them had their names on their golf bags and their initials on their head covers. It also seemed as if everybody was color-coordinated—

clothes, bags, head covers. One family published a newsletter, supposedly about junior golf, that was actually a thinly disguised promotional brochure touting their fifteen-year-old son.

When I had the chance, I took Nancy aside. "We may have made a big mistake coming here," I told her. "We're way out of our league with these people. Some of these kids have *teaching pros*."

"Do you think Danny's going to be intimidated?" she asked.

"I don't know," I said. "But I sure am."

I felt better after we were treated graciously by the tournament director, Nan Ryan, but I was still a bit apprehensive about being there.

Danny apparently did not share my apprehension, he finished fourth out of a field of about 30 ten- and eleven-year-olds. He was in contention to win his age group until a three-putt resulted in a double-bogie late in the last round. He played well. More importantly, though, he conducted himself properly—even when he made a mistake. We were very proud parents.

On the way back to Grand Haven, the three of us discussed the experience and Danny's relative success. Nancy and I were curious to learn whether or not he was nervous or felt any pressure from the kids he played with or the parents in the gallery. Or both. I suppose we should have expected his answer.

"Pressure?" he replied. "That's not pressure. *Pressure* is standing over a ten-foot, downhill putt in the backyard for the family championship. With your brothers standing in stone silence, *praying* to all the gods of golf for you to miss. *That's* pressure."

Nancy and I both had to laugh.

When we found out that the West Michigan Amateur golf tournament was going to be held at our home course, Danny asked if he could enter. I checked to see if there was an age limit and found there was only a handicap limit and Danny qualified. He didn't play as well as he could have on the first day, unfortunately, but his 36-hole total of 176 (89-77) put him just below the middle of the pack and earned him a photo in the *Grand Rapids Press*.

Over the next few years, Danny blossomed. And as he grew he became stronger and was able to hit the golf ball farther and with more versatility. In hockey, he got faster and more agile. In baseball, he developed a strong arm and more foot speed, and he learned to hit with power. I knew he was good, but, thinking about it now, there were a couple of instances that should have given me a clue that my youngest son was a bit more than just your average athlete.

When he was eleven and playing in a baseball championship game at Ferrysburg school, our team was batting in the last inning, trailing by one run. Danny was scheduled to be the fourth batter in the inning. Apparently, the opposing manager knew this, too. I heard him tell his pitcher, Mike Wilson, to get the first three batters out because "You don't want to face Danny Bylsma in this situation."

After two outs, the third batter reached base and gave Danny a chance to hit. The opposing manager quickly called time-out and went out to the mound. I couldn't tell what they were talking about, but I knew that the league's rules did not allow intentional walks. I suspected an "unintentional" intentional walk was being called for.

Danny hit Mike's first pitch well over the left field fence—but about ten feet foul. The next pitch was called a ball. Danny sent the third pitch over the left field fence—this time, just inches foul. Another ball put the count at two-and-two. On the next pitch there was no doubt. The ball sailed well over the center field fence.

Then there was the time Danny was invited by a friend to sleep over one Friday night. The friend had entered a Shoot, Pass and Dribble basketball contest that was to be held the next morning at the local YMCA. I told Danny I would pick him up at the "Y" after the contest. I got there in time to watch his friend compete but what I saw, instead, was Danny win the competition in his age group. Afterward, I told him I didn't know he had signed up.

"I didn't," he replied. "But when I got here they asked if I wanted to enter. So I thought: 'I'm here. Might as well.'"

"Basketball is not exactly your sport," I said. "How did you know what to do?"

Danny shrugged his shoulders. "I made sure I wasn't the first one to compete in each event so I could see how other guys did the drills and what it took to win."

I had a passing moment of jealousy. When I was in the eighth grade, I had earned a blue ribbon for coming in first in the broad jump in an inter-city track meet. One blue ribbon in a lifetime. My son, on the other hand, had enough raw athletic ability—along with competitive intelligence—to win events he didn't plan on entering and in sports he didn't even play. More than that, the competition in our backyard had taught him to identify what it took to excel and to win. When he went outside that environment, evidently that knowledge went with him.

I am convinced this ability helped him in other ways. He developed a sense of what it took to get good grades. He also seemed to know how to ingratiate himself with his teachers and coaches. As far as I can remember, Danny did not have a teacher or a coach—at any level—who was not fond of him.

When Danny was eleven, he went back to the Little People's Golf Tournament and set a record with an even-par score of 36 on the front nine. He faltered a bit on the back with a 41. His 77 placed him second by one stroke. Until it was broken in 1996, his nine-hole scoring record stood for fourteen years.

Every year—with each sport he played—I saw that Danny was noticeably better at the start of each season than I remembered him being at the end of the previous one. I think it was because he always played at the limit of his physical ability. That is, what his body would allow him to do. When he came back to a sport after a five- or six-month layoff, he had grown taller, gotten stronger and smarter and, therefore, had passed his previous limitations.

Nancy and I thought it was because God had given him special gifts.

As were all the children, he was growing up emotionally as well. After being there for the kids, we felt the next most important necessity for child-rearing was clear rules that were consistently applied. In that regard, we were almost inflexible.

• Church services and church related activities came before sports and almost everything else short of eating and sleeping. And when a youth group put on a musical or some other kind of a program, the children were expected to participate. I remember Scott doing a stand-up comedy routine imitating Richard Nixon and John Wayne for a variety show. Jon played an outstanding Nebuchadnezzar in a musical. Another time the kids and I sang in a talent show for the sole purpose of getting Nancy to come up on stage, ostensibly so she could put a pie in my face. To her surprise, she got one in the face, too. How the boys fought for that honor!

• The importance of education was just under the import of religion. It was assumed you would attempt to be at, or near, the head of your class in academics. To be a good athlete, you needed the ability to think clearly and decisively. That was what school taught you. College was a given. Also, unlimited athletic participation was the reward that came to those who did their best in school.

• All of our children had to learn, or at least *attempt* to learn, a musical instrument. Since I had sung in a barbershop quartet in high school, my dream was to spawn the Bylsma equivalent of the Osmond Brothers. Unfortunately it turned out that music wasn't their forte. Wisely, we switched our expectations from singing to instruments. Scott butchered the trombone for one year (an unfortunate choice because you need an ear to play the trombone). Greg took two years to learn to play chopsticks badly on the piano (I still wonder if his teacher's decision to quit giving lessons had anything to do with her lack of success with him). Jon attempted the clarinet, and Danny attempted the drums. The only musical success was Laurie who played piano and sang in the high school choir.

• You had to learn the rules of the games you played and respect the officials. A knowledge of the rules kept you from making unwitting mistakes and allowed you the opportunity to use them to your advantage. The umpire was not always right . . . but he was always the umpire. All of the boys took turns at umpiring Kids League baseball and softball, and some of them refereed hockey—Jon, all the way up to the college level.

When he was thirteen, Danny came home after umpiring a baseball game of ten-year-olds and told us, "You might as well hear it from me. I threw one of the managers out of the game."

"You threw a manager out? What happened?"

"There was a close play at third base," he said, "and I thought the runner was out. This loudmouth father-slash-manager thought his player was safe and went into a rage to try to intimidate me. He got in my face and said some things that would have gotten me a Palmolive cocktail. After he had gone on for more than long enough, I got up enough courage to tell him that I thought I had called the play right. Furthermore, I had heard enough from him and if he kept it up I would have to throw him out of the game. Then I went back to home plate.

"Getting told by a thirteen-year-old that he might get thrown out of a game must have ignited him because he went off like a rocket. He started back in on me with a vengeance. I was cornered and there was no place to run. I had just told a grown man I would throw him out if he kept screaming at me and now he was doing just that. So I raised my thumb above my head and said, 'You . . . are outta here.' If I thought he was mad before, I was wrong."

"He didn't leave the park?" I asked.

"No, he went behind the backstop and continued to heckle me," Danny said. "So I held up the game and tried to glare at him. Thank goodness a parent from his team convinced him to go to his car or he'd still be yelling at me and I'd still be trying to glare at him. I umpired the rest of the game just shaking in my boots."

The discipline of umpiring and refereeing gave each of the boys a lifelong appreciation for the officiating profession.

• Mom and Dad are the arbitrators and mete out punishments. We didn't allow the kids to hit each other. We always told them: if you want to hit children, have some of your own; don't hit ours.

• Your word was your honor and your honor was sacred. You never lied. The kids were given slaps on the wrist for goofing off; serious punishments for lying.

• Mom and Dad would provide what you *need*; you must pay half for something you *want*. If you want new skates when you don't need new skates, you pay half the cost for new ones. Or, Mom and Dad will pay for adequate skates, you pay the extra if you want top-of-the-line skates.

• You never forgot the Eleventh Commandment. For those of you who mistakenly think there are only the ten commandments given by God to Moses on Mount Sinai, let me enlighten you as to the Eleventh. It is "Thou shalt not bullshit thy father."

This "commandment" caused me no little embarrassment when five-year-old Jon's Sunday School teacher, a very proper lady, told me that she had told her kindergarten class about the Ten Commandments the previous Sunday (". . . skipping quickly over the seventh, of course," she whispered). When she had finished Jon raised his little hand to inform her that there were eleven commandments.

"No, Jon," the teacher explained, "God only gave us ten commandments."

"My dad says there are eleven," insisted Jon.

It was here, the teacher told me, that she made her fatal mistake. "He was so adamant, I just had to ask him what his father said was this extra commandment."

With confidence and obvious pride, and to the dear lady's horror, the little guy told her. "Thou shalt not bullshit thy father."

Nancy said she wished she could have been a mouse in the corner of that classroom.

Our rules are easy to summarize, though not always easy to enforce:

- A person needs a moral standard and an accountability to a higher being. For us, it is the Judeo-Christian God.
- Education is a possession to be valued above wealth, and it often creates a quality of life that is almost impossible to achieve without it.
- Have balance in your life and appreciate the arts.
- Live and play by the rules and respect the authority that enforces them.
- Live with integrity and honor.
- As smart as you think you are at age thirteen, your parents were that smart thirty years ago; borrow from their experience and wisdom, but rebel against it at your own peril.
- Wants are different than needs.

Those were the rules for the kids . . . so what were the rules for the parents? Love the kids a lot, support them a lot, pray for them a lot, worry about them a lot, and be sure they are aware of the extent of your love, support, prayers, and concern for them.

Having said that, an obvious question may be: Why did we allow so much participation in sports? What do sports have to do with life? The answer—as the hundreds of kids who have had me as a coach heard every year—is this: Sports are a microcosm of life.

Let me explain by using hockey as a model. Everyone brings to the rink his prior experience and his talent (everything he has become at that moment). The extent to which he has prepared himself will, in large measure, determine his success. There are coaches (parents and teachers in life) who teach him the game (educate him) and the rules to play by (just as there are rules to live by). There are referees (policemen and judges in life) to enforce the rules and impose penalties if there are infractions (fines and, perhaps, jail in life). Success in the game (and life) will be largely determined by one's ability to combine experience, talent, preparation, hard work, coaching, and playing within the rules. Sometimes sports are not fair. Sometimes life is not fair. Sports are models of life that an eight-year-old can be taught and understand with great clarity because the cause and effects are immediate and obvious.

The application of sports as a model for teaching life's lessons is valid for kids irrespective of athletic ability. By the time our daughter was approaching the age requirement for playing Kids League baseball, the president of the league led the way in adding girls' softball to the program. When Laurie heard there was going to be girls' softball, she looked up at me with her big blue eyes and said, "You coached the boys when they played, you're going to coach me now, aren't you, Daddy?" If I could write it the way she asked it, you would understand why I couldn't turn her down— even if I had wanted to. That same doe-eyed look and raised eyebrow technique has been good for a lot of stuff and services ever since.

Over the three years that I coached girls' softball, they received instruction in the fundamentals, learned how to read signs from their third base coach, and got lessons in the rules of the game—as well as life. Quite a few of these girls became good high school players and several went on to play college ball. While Laurie only played a little in high school, the life lessons she learned are as much a part of her as they are of the boys. These life lessons have helped her socially as well as professionally.

In case I'm beginning to sound like a pompous ass who thinks he knows everything, which my family and friends will attest I don't, let me relate another story about my best intentions going awry. It's a story that my kids repeat all too often to their friends.

The boys were often restless and distracted during services at our church. My thought was that if you could sit in rapt attention in front of the TV for two hours watching a football game, you could sit and at least *pretend* to pay attention for one hour in church. Time and time again I was wrong and, believe me, I tried every sort of punishment—from depriving them of watching their beloved Detroit Lions' football game on Sunday afternoon, to sitting in a chair for an hour. Nothing worked.

One year, around Easter, I got a flash of inspiration. I took Scott, who was about twelve at the time, up to one of the bedrooms and expressed my displeasure at his restless behavior in church and how it bothered the worshippers around us. Prior punishments had been to no avail, I told him, and it hurt me to have to punish him, but actions had consequences and someone had to pay the price. So, I said—and at that point I began taking off my shirt—if he would take this small bat and administer to me the punishment he thought was fair . . . just like Jesus, I would take the punishment in his place.

Scott immediately melted into tears and began blubbering about how he couldn't hit me and how sorry he was. My immediate thought was: I may be onto something!

Same song, second verse with Greg; same teary-eyed response to my little performance, followed by the very welcome, "I'll never do it again, Dad." Now I was *certain* I was onto something.

Jon is next and he gets the same song, third verse. As I am bending over the bed, preparing to take the punishment I'm sure won't come, I hear a sound that I later determined to be the sound of someone spitting into his hands and rubbing them together, as if to get a better grip on something. It was just an instant before Jon almost broke my back with the business end of the Little League bat.

Since then, the boys have frequently warned me not to give them another opportunity to participate in my Jesus act.

DAN

As I reflect back on my early childhood, it's difficult to pick out any clear path that my parents may have wanted my brothers, sister and me to follow. What is clear is that the central themes that were important to my parents were made central in the lives of their children.

My parents centered our family around their religious beliefs. Church, Sunday school, and the Christian day school were important in our family life *and* in the life of each child. My parents lived their lives in respect of the ultimate reality of God, and religion and the church were at the center of their lives and our family.

Even though I was a young boy at the time, I can still remember my older brothers getting help on their homework. I can still see my dad sitting at the kitchen table assisting with a math or English assignment. School and that attention was something that I yearned for and all too soon received. In my recollection, school was the single most important thing that I did in my parent's view, especially at report card time. Before looking at the grades, my Dad would hold up the card and say, "Is this the best you can do? Did you work as hard as possible to get these grades?" If the answer was yes, he'd say, "Then I'm proud of your work." Sometimes, he would just hand the card back to me. More often than not, though, we would review the grades together.

My parents used the dinner table to stress the importance of family and our individual roles in it. The dinner table was a time the whole family spent together—no exceptions—and the TV was not allowed to be on while we ate. Each one of us was expected to share the events of his day. When I was younger, I had to be quick to get a second helping, as well as a word in edgewise. The tradition continues when we get together now; family meals can run more than two hours, as everyone is expected to share the events of their lives since they last were at the table together. I wonder if it was by chance that more than occasionally the dinner table discussion focused on religious, philosophical, or ethical questions. Dinner time was a learning time, a sharing time.

A vivid memory remains of one such dinner. Laurie was in the second grade and Greg was a junior in high school. He had been given a sociology class assignment to list all of the things that boys could do better than girls. Apparently, it was an assignment intended to teach something about the equality of the sexes. Greg had several examples on his list and my other brothers and I added several more. At dinner the next night, he couldn't wait to tell us about the results of the discussion in his sociology class.

To each example of superiority that the students offered, the teacher pointed out someone of the opposite sex who had equal ability. For example, when a girl asserted that women were better cooks, the teacher countered with the fact that most chefs were men. Apparently, the lesson of the day was lost on Greg.

"I got so mad," he told us, "that I finally raised my hand and said that I knew something that boys could do better than girls. When she asked me what it was, I said, 'Write our name in the snow.' And then some girl said that *she* could write her name in the snow. Can you just see that?" he asked us. Whereupon, he got up from the table, squatted down and proceeded to scuttle about the dining room as if he were a girl in the process of "writing" her name in the snow. We were laughing so hard we just about choked on our food.

But then, in that quiet moment that often follows a lot of laughter, we heard little Laurie say: "She would have to do it in cursive."

We almost died laughing.

The privilege of going out to play, participating in sports, or just about anything else revolved around mastering our schoolwork. All other activities were delayed until schoolwork was given proper attention. That is, all other activities except those that were church related.

To the Bylsma children, "all other activities" most often meant sports. From the time I could put one foot in front of the other, I emulated some of the best competitors I would ever know—my brothers. By that I mean that Scott's hockey skills were obviously more advanced than mine—he was nine years older—and the difference in our skill level was greater than, say, Jaromir Jagr's skills compared to mine now. When I line up against Jagr now, I think: "I've been here before." The difference is that I eventually caught up to Scott.

While my parents were raising us to have the values that were the center of their own lives, my brothers were instilling in me the value of competition. My emulation of them started at a very young age, and as I grew there was nothing I wanted more than to be a part of the games they played. When my abilities caught up to my desire, they allowed me to progress from full-time catcher in baseball (I caught for both teams but didn't get to bat)or full-time center in football (I hiked the ball to both quarterbacks) into being a competitor.

Although having and maintaining a real golf green and an ice rink in our backyard was a lot of hard work for the whole family, it was a place not only for our family but the whole neighborhood to play. To this day, people we hardly remember come up and reminisce about the good times they had playing in our backyard. Was this backyard playground my parents' way of pushing us? No, it was their way of keeping their eye on us.

As we grew older, the games evolved. At first, our "golf course" was from sprinkler head to the bird feeder, from the bird feeder to the tall oak, and so on. However, as our skills progressed and our imagination grew, so did our venues. Whether it was our first imaginary golf course or later on our homemade green, our "tour events" began to coincide with the PGA's tour events. When the U.S. Open rolled around with its notoriously long roughs, our parents would let us suspend mowing the lawn for two weeks. Our U.S. Open course consisted of mowed tees and greens with dangerously long rough. We dried out the grass for our version of the British Open and the victor of the Masters got to write his name on a cherished green sweatshirt. There were proud moments getting interviewed after winning a tournament, especially a major, and telling the assembled throng (your brothers) how you managed to grab victory from the jaws of defeat.

I learned quickly that it was great to win but less satisfying to lose. I also learned that there were games within each game; one-on-one situations—you against one of the other players—and that one's performance in these situations could contribute to your side winning the game. That was how I learned how to be a team player.

My emulation of my brothers carried into my high school years. Scott and Greg had played high school golf and I couldn't wait to try my luck. I had also watched Scott and Greg play on the baseball team in high school so I hoped to make the team myself. Not only did I want to follow in their footsteps, I wanted to perform better than they did.

Scott's going away to college had a profound effect on me. He attended Bowling Green State University on a partial golf scholarship and with hopes of playing hockey as well. Scott made the hockey team as a walk-on, but didn't play his freshman year. Nonetheless, going to BG to see his team play and meet some of his teammates quickly made a Falcon fan out of me. My hero worship of Scott reached new levels and my favorite colors became seal brown and burnt orange, those of Bowling Green.

It was tough to consider myself a good athlete when three of my competitors had skills so much superior to my own. Due to their mentoring, however, such stiff competition turned out to be an inspiration and not a discouragement. I never felt the pressure of having to live up to the accomplishments of my brothers. I just wanted to be good enough to compete in the backyard, in the driveway, or wherever the venue was for the next particular donnybrook.

The themes of church, education, and family were administered by two standards: Hard work and doing your best are the ingredients for improvement and higher achievement; there were rules to live and play by, and there were consequences if you didn't choose to do so.

One of the few expectations that my parents had of me and my siblings was to apply our best effort to whatever task was at hand, whether it was schoolwork, chores, sports, or the church musical. The surprising consequence was that we learned that how well you performed in school or in sports was a direct result of how much effort went into the activity. I learned that success and achieving goals came through practice and hard work.

I also found that if I worked hard, help was available. It was an easy lesson to learn because my Dad was always willing to go into the backyard and hit ground balls or play catch or help with math assignments. I still don't know who enjoyed the experience more—Dad or me.

Improving was something you wanted to do—you needed to do—when you have three older brothers who wouldn't give an inch in the backyard pickup games. The best players usually won. In order to be one of the best players, I needed to improve. Improving required working hard. Thus, if you wanted to experience the fun of winning, you needed to work hard. Simple.

My parents didn't harp on their children to always work harder and harder still. The lesson my parents taught us was that the results weren't as important as being able to say you have done your best. If you had given your best effort, then no matter what the results, you could hold your head up and be proud.

The value of this wisdom was made very clear at age eleven during my second year at the Little People's Golf Tournament. On the first day of the tournament, I shot an even par 36—a record score for my age group—and found myself in the lead by two strokes. Never did I make more new friends in such a short time than after I set that record. Adults and kids alike came up to say hello and offer congratulations and advice. The following day, however, I didn't play as well and slipped to second place. I found that not only had I lost the tournament . . . but each and every one of my new friends as well. The disappointment brought tears.

My parents' usual response ("Did you give your best effort? Then we're proud of you.") offered me little consolation at the time. But later, after the tears had dried, the lesson of doing your best and giving your all, began to motivate me to work harder. That tournament also taught me that there was a mental part of sports and that the mental handling of losing was as fundamental as handling the fun of winning. Mental is as much a part of "fundamental" as is fun.

Around the Bylsma house it was very clear how law and order was kept. There were rules. If you broke the rules, you dealt with your father and he didn't suffer scofflaws lightly. His looks of displeasure were usually enough to send me into third degree contrition.

I am sure my first experience outside the rules was well before my memory kicks in. But I wasn't very old before I understood what was expected and that there were unpleasant consequences if your behavior fell short of expectations.

I do have one all too vivid memory of a time when I was eight years old and I tried to lie my way out of being caught with baseball cards I had stolen from the Pickle Barrel, a local convenience store. After lying myself into a hole that I couldn't get out of, I found myself in the family car with my father. He drove me back to Pickle Barrel and I had to apologize to the stern-looking manager who decided—at what seemed like the last moment—not to call the police. Back at home, I learned that one way to clean out a mouth that spoke such lies was with liquid dishwashing detergent. A Palmolive cocktail, and being on the very brink of a long-term jail sentence, turned out to be a fairly effective way to prevent further lying and stealing.

For not getting along with brothers and sisters, the penalty was a little more theatrical. The culprits were made to face the music of my father's considerable rhetoric, lined-up in front of the sofa, bending over with our hands resting on the back cushions. It was as effective a position as bending over to touch your toes but more stable and not quite as humiliating. Once positioned, a stern lecture about what we had done wrong followed. Typically, this verbal tirade would include scary words and phrases such as, "These war-like behaviors and acrimonious attitudes will no longer be tolerated . . . " or "Your contumacious behavior has succeeded in pushing your mother's patience far beyond all reasonable limits and you have pushed me to the point of apoplexy . . . " and it took me years to fully understand them. An admonition as to how our behavior was expected to improve would follow, along with a rap on the behind with an old broom handle to drive the message home, so to speak. While " . . . this hurts me more than it hurts you" and "I'm doing this for your own good" rarely salved our injured egos or took the sting out of the rap, the rules and expectations of childhood and being part of a family have definitely left a mark on me (and not just on my butt). Rules are in place for reasons, obvious or subtle, known or unknown, and breaking the rules always brings consequences, foreseen or unforeseen, sooner or later.

As athletics always took a back seat to church, school, and even the dinner table, sports came after each of these were given proper attention, rarely before. My parents made sure we had time for church youth group, piano lessons, band and choir, and the other activities that made you a well-rounded person. Sports was a privilege received after you had made an appropriate effort at being well-rounded.

Today, the conventional wisdom seems to be that the only way to develop good athletic skills is to play a single sport all year round. My parents held the opposite opinion and I agree with it. They didn't raise

me to be a hockey player. My siblings and I were encouraged to participate in every sport offered by our schools and in our community. Baseball, golf, soccer, basketball, hockey, and flag football (not tackle football; that was considered too dangerous) were sports that we couldn't wait to play when their respective seasons came around. Looking back, playing a variety of sports developed us into well-rounded athletes. Each sport focused on different skills that, generally, were applicable to the others.

Playing baseball helped me to understand the importance of playing my position in hockey. My dad (also my coach at the time) once asked a teammate who didn't understand this importance if he had ever seen a first baseman run over to third base to field a ground ball. The visual image of that example made a lasting impression on all of us. The mechanics necessary for shooting a puck in hockey or hitting a baseball translates very well into hitting a golf ball. The offensive and defensive setup in basketball (two forwards, a center, and two guards/defensemen) is a close parallel to hockey (except goaltending is frowned upon in basketball).

Even though it is the current conventional wisdom to have children focus on one sport, parents typically don't decide for a child at age nine or ten that he or she will be a doctor so that they can focus all their studies on medicine.

In regard to my siblings and me, our developed skills have carried over into varied activities as we have matured. My brothers continue to be outstanding golfers and this ability has been an asset in both social and professional situations. Scott's ability to drive a golf ball into tomorrow has led to some enviable invitations (to play at Pebble Beach in some very select company, for example) and many of his clients are also golfing acquaintances. Jon was a member of his firm's team in the Grand Rapids Bar Association's annual golf championship. At the end of eighteen holes they were tied with another team and the championship was to be decided by a long drive contest. With one hundred members of the Bar standing by, Jon drove last and hit a three hundred yard drive with a three-wood to beat one of the best amateur golfers in town. Jon hopes that eventually his peers will remember him as much for his legal skills as they now do for his ability to hit a golf ball.

My childhood memories are dominated by the knowledge that I was a welcomed member of a tight-knit family. My parents loved me unconditionally while demanding that I do my best. My brothers were, at times, my greatest opponents while they were my greatest heroes. I learned that hard work paid off, while losing was not much fun. Pushing myself to the next level started with the lessons learned at home, but it wasn't work really—it was fun.

The whole time I was growing up, never once did my parents ever say that my goal should be the NHL or major league baseball or the PGA or being a doctor or a C.P.A. Family, church, school, sports; tools to develop a God-fearing, intelligent, educated, contributing member of society. The NHL? Not a hint.

2

HIGH SCHOOL

JAY

It was during his high school years that we really began to think that perhaps Dan was more than just your average good athlete and that his skills might take him beyond Grand Haven, Michigan. Since the elementary school he attended and the high school it fed both had ninth grades, he had a choice of either. We felt the academics were the same. Athletics-wise, he would either be a big fish in a small pool at the elementary school or a small fish in a big pool at the high school. In the end, partly because Jon was going to be a senior, we decided to send Dan to the high school for the ninth grade. We thought he might be ready to compete in high school sports.

Within days of the start of the school season, the high school varsity golf program began. Jon had been the runner-up for state medalist the year before and although Danny could usually beat Jon, Dan didn't play up to his potential that fall. Besides, it was comfortable being #2 behind his brother, a senior that year. Fortunately, the team managed to qualify for the state finals that were held at the Webberville (MI) Country Club.

The day before the state tournament, Jon, Danny, and I played a practice round at WCC. Jon hit the ball well but Dan struggled with his swing as he had all season. I felt that Jon would have a good chance to better his second place finish of the previous year but that Dan would just have to use the tournament as a learning experience.

The next day, I walked with Dan for several holes thinking he could use the support. He was not hitting his drives well and was scrambling. But he was making pars, for the most part. After I felt that Dan had settled in, I followed Jon for a while. Jon was hitting the ball well but was letting strokes slip away. When Jon began playing the back nine, I heard that someone had played the front nine in evenpar. I decided to find Dan to see how he was doing. When I saw him, he gave me a hand signal to indicate that he was evenpar. I wasn't sure if he meant for the round or for just the back nine, but I was very surprised because of how he'd been struggling earlier.

I watched him two-putt for par on the par-four 15th, then scramble for par on the par-three 16th. The boys' golf coach, Vern Nyhoff, caught up to me at that point and told me that Dan had shot two over par on the front nine and he was pretty sure he was evenpar on the back. Dan reached the green on the par-five 17th hole in three and sunk a forty-foot birdie putt to go to one over par for his round.

At the dog-leg-right par-four 18th hole, Dan sliced his drive into the right rough near a huge weeping willow tree. Two small maple trees stood between him and the hole and there was a bunker guarding his approach to the green. I remarked to the coach that he was stymied because I couldn't see how he could get the ball up quick enough to avoid the closest maple. It seemed to me that the smart play was to pitch out to the fairway in hopes of chipping it close enough for a one-putt par. Even a bogey would give him a 74 and that might be good enough for a first place tie and possibly even the medal.

Dan pulled out a club and lined up to go right for the pin. I cringed. The odds for a successful shot were small and disaster loomed. But he struck the ball without hesitation and got it up quickly enough to miss the maple. After it landed just over the bunker, it rolled to within five feet of the pin. Dan's successful birdie putt, following such an amazing shot, almost seemed anticlimactic. His even par score of 72 was the low round by two strokes. It was the first time a freshman had ever won the state championship.

The first person to give Dan a giant hug was his brother. Jon had shot 78 and later said, "If I couldn't win it, I desperately wanted Danny to get it." The first person Dan wanted to call was his oldest brother. Scott was in his senior year at Bowling Green and was playing hockey in Sault Ste. Marie (MI) against Lake Superior State. "I got the medal, Grizz," Danny told him.

Considering that he had struggled through most of his round, I was impressed by how he had won the championship. Simply put: he did what it took to win. Watching him, I saw a different person than I thought I knew. I couldn't help but think of the expression, "My kid grew up right under my nose." Dan had turned fourteen only a month before, but seemed to have matured right in front of me. Over the eighteen holes, he was all business and concentration. He was poised and decisive. From the 15th hole on, he exuded a serene, quiet self-confidence that was evident to me and to the players in his group and the coaches who were watching. One of the coaches, upon learning from his senior player in Dan's foursome that Dan was in ninth grade, exclaimed, "That kid is just a freshman?" To which the player replied, "Trust me, he's not just a freshman—he's a machine. It wouldn't have mattered what I shot, he would have beat me." Clearly, Dan had learned how to win the one-on-one.

When they awarded the medals, the presenting coach pointed out that Scott had been Medalist in 1980, Greg the Runner-up in 1982, Jon the Runner-up in 1983, and that Dan had followed in the remarkable tradition his brothers had set. I was more than a little proud. But I also couldn't help but reflect on all the practice, all the hard work that resulted in their achievements. Hitting shots to our backyard green from thirty yards out until three went into the hole, then moving to forty yards . . . all the maintenance the green required, the lugging of hoses for watering, the mixing of insecticides and fungicides, the pesky moles, the many trips to the Crockery Hills, Silver Lake, and Grand Haven Golf courses—all of it was worth it. And I'd do it all over again in a heartbeat. Because they won? No, winning was only incidental to the importance of the way it helped them mature, gain confidence in themselves, and come to understand how much work and effort it takes to become successful.

Sports is a microcosm of life.

Hockey that year was not everything we had hoped it would be. Several of the best players in the league decided to play travel hockey out of Grand Rapids. At the same time, a group of parents of younger players had been meeting to get travel hockey started in the Muskegon area. Through their efforts, the Muskegon Chiefs—a quasi-travel teams of Squirts, Pee Wees, Bantams, and Midgets—came into being.

Dan and Jon were asked to play for the Midget team. The team did not belong to a league, but a twenty-game schedule had been arranged, including some tournaments and games against Grand Rapids high school teams. The coach was a young man who, at that time, probably lacked the maturity to deal with high school kids. Before long, officials asked if I would be willing to take the team over, and I was back at coaching. Dan was approaching Jon in size, speed, and ability. When I could get them on the ice together, they were a joy to watch.

As hockey season wound down, the high school baseball season began and Dan went out for the team. The coach was Joe Hicks, assisted by Sam DeBoer. Greg had played for Sam in his senior year and had a very good experience. He had been the team's MVP. I felt good about Sam as a coach and was certain that Dan would get a fair shot.

As the pre-season practices wore on, Dan became optimistic that he was good enough to not only make the team—freshman or not—but to play. He was hitting the ball well and as he said, "There are fielding positions that are not solid." However, in a team meeting before the start of the season, Joe Hicks announced that if you were a freshman and made the team, you shouldn't count on playing much. The seniors on the team had been coming to practice for three and four years and had earned the right to play.

I asked Dan how he felt about that philosophy. He was undeterred. "There are *seniors* who can't hit the ball," he said. "Some of them aren't so hot in the field, either."

"How are *you* doing?" I asked.

"I'm hitting the ball good, and I can field with any of them."

"Well, bide your time and keep a good attitude," I said. "When the time comes, and it will, be ready to make the best of it." Hadn't I once said the same thing to Scott?

"I'll be ready," Dan said.

And he was. When the season started, Dan was used in a pinch-hitting role and managed to hit the ball well. Then West Michigan Christian High (W.M.C.H.) went up against Calvin Christian and had to face Ken Komejan, their all-state pitcher. Komejan was cruising along with a no-hitter when Dan came up as a pinch hitter in the sixth inning. He lined a curve ball to right field to get the only hit of the day for W.M.C.H. That hit, coupled with some sloppy play in the outfield by the regulars, earned Dan a starting spot in left field.

As the season wore on, he gained more confidence. Being the youngest player on a team was not new to Dan. In spite of his age, he became a leader and an inspiration to his teammates. The Detroit Tigers had won the World Series the year before and Dan had obtained a poster that replicated the front page of *The Detroit Free Press*. It included a photo of Tiger star Kirk Gibson, leaping into the air after hitting a decisive home run. Dan took the poster to every game and hung it inside the dugout. He looked up to Gibson and admired his work ethic and desire to win. Even today, he carries a small picture of "Gibby" in his wallet.

Dan changed the language of the team. A hard line drive was a "Gibby shot." If a player needed some talisman or extra effort, Dan would bestow "the power of Gibb" or give him "the Gibby blessing." If someone dared mock this homage, Dan would put on a serious face and chastise the mocker with, "Hey, you don't blaspheme Gibby unless you're better than Gibby. And you ain't better than Gibby!"

Since Dan seemed to have "the power of Gibb" himself, very few of his teammates blasphemed. In the state tournament, Dan played key roles. On June 1, 1985, the Muskegon *Chronicle* reported:

> *Coach Joe Hicks' Warriors made up a 4–3 deficit with four tallies in the sixth on Dan Bylsma's two run double and Dolislager's triple which chased in two more.*

The following week, the Sunday *Chronicle* carried this headline:

Christian's Warriors Earn Trip to State Semifinals

The accompanying article said: *"WM Christian 6 Beal City 2. Down 2–1 in the top of the last inning, Christian kept its cool and it paid off as two runners reached on errors after pitcher John Maeder had retired the leadoff man. Freshman Dan Bylsma wasn't about to let a good thing pass his team. He doubled in the tying run with his second hit of the game.*

Then later in the article:

> *WM Christian 8, Marion 2—Christian settled the issue in the first inning with a six-run outburst which featured five consecutive hits. Bylsma's RBI triple started the uprising . . .*

It wasn't just Dan's bat that made him an impact player. W.M.C.H. had reached the state semifinals to face a very good Bear Lake High School team. The *Chronicle* article about the victory over Bear Lake carried this paragraph:

> *. . . three defensive plays also gave the Warriors, now 15–10, the nod. One came when Bear Lake's leading hitter, Joe Ledford overslid third during a two-run rally in the sixth. Shortstop Keith TerHaar closed out an inning with a grab of a hot grounder with two Laker runners in scoring position while freshman standout Dan Bylsma made a one-handed running*

catch of a bid for a lead-off double by Sanderson in the seventh to avert major trouble . . .

So the W.M.C.H. Warriors qualified for the state baseball finals in Class D. In an editorial in the Muskegon *Chronicle*, Sports Editor Mart Tardani wrote about the players the Warrior coaching staff expected to play a major role in the team's chances for victory:

(Coaches) Hicks and DeBoer hope Dan Bylsma, the team's biggest surprise, keeps up the good work.

Bylsma has already earned the nickname of "Mr. Icicle Veins" for his clutch hitting.

"When we need a big hit, he doesn't choke at all. He does the job. As you know, Dan got the key blow of the game when we beat Beal City in the last inning of our regional opener. You won't find too many freshmen who can do what he has already done for us," said Hicks of the 5-11, 170 (lb.) frosh find.

The final was washed out and delayed until the following Monday afternoon. This presented a problem for Dan who had been invited to attend the Michigan Select Bantam hockey camp which ran from that Monday through Friday. The top sixty ranked thirteen- and fourteen-year-olds from the state were invited to Houghton, Michigan, for a week-long camp from which sixteen players would be selected to attend the USA Select Bantam Camp in Colorado Springs.

Dan decided to play in the state final on Monday, and Nancy agreed to leave after the game and drive the twelve-hour trip to Houghton so Dan could be there for Tuesday's session.

The day after the Class D baseball championship, the Muskegon *Chronicle* carried several stories about the Warriors' 5–4 victory over Grass Lake High School. According to the Sports Editor, Dan played an important part in the victory.

. . . Freshman Dan Bylsma then lashed his second hit of the game to plate Jesse Jaeger, who had walked and swiped second.

I have quoted the newspaper because if I told the story in my own words, it could occur to you that I am an aggrandizing father. But, as you have read, he had a career year in baseball—as a freshman. Time after time there were game-winning hits (Gibby shots), important stolen bases, and great defensive plays. He wound up with twenty-five hits in sixty-three at bats for a .397 batting average. He had fifteen RBIs and thirteen stolen bases in thirteen attempts. He was awarded first team All-Conference, All-District, and All-Regional.

He led by example. He worked hard, he hustled, he hit, he scored—he was everywhere. His teammates were forced to deal with his level of enthusiasm and hard work. If this freshman could do it, the other players were called upon to rise to a new level of achievement.

I would pick him up each day from practice and on the way home we would stop at Sluka Field, a baseball field near our home. He would go into center field and I would hit fly balls to him—one hundred and fifty to two hundred of them. I would hit them to left-center and I would hit them to right-center. He would then position himself in shallow center field and I would try to hit the fly balls over his head. After that, he would go to deep center field and I would try to hit them short.

I would hit balls until my hands began to blister and I would beg to stop. He'd holler, "Just one more to my right." That "... *one-handed running catch of a bid for a lead-off double*" in the semifinal game against Bear Lake High School? Truth be known, Dan had made similar catches, and others more difficult, a thousand times before in our "games" at Sluka Field.

Nancy, Laurie, and Dan left the celebration following the championship game and headed for Houghton. I was left at home to wonder how Dan would do against hockey players his own age. I thought he might have a chance to be invited to Colorado Springs. He wasn't invited, but he was only a first year Bantam so it was likely there were second year Bantams who were better than Dan.

The first time I talked to Nancy, I asked her how she thought he looked compared to the other players. Her reply was significant, although I didn't understand why at the time. "I thought he was one of the best kids on the ice," she told me, "but I don't always know what I'm looking at."

During the summer, I reflected on what Danny had accomplished during his first year in high school athletics. He had been the state medalist in golf, he had surpassed his brother Jon in hockey (a senior and a very good hockey player in his own right), and he had led his team to a state championship in baseball.

I began to think that he was someone special, that God had given him special gifts. The scary part was that God had given him to Nancy and me. I wondered how we could help him, what he would eventually become, and where would it all end up. I said to myself over and over, "Danny, Danny. What will become of you?"

I knew I didn't have to worry about him gaining a sense of self-importance. It didn't matter what he had accomplished; one of his brothers had done it before him and they were not afraid to remind him of his position in the family—dead last. At the same time, they reveled in his achievements and rightly so. They had been his mentors and role models and were, perhaps, more responsible for his success than anyone.

It was a great family in which to be the father. Golf changed to Saturday afternoon at Grand Haven Golf Club—a tough, tree lined course that's ranked one of the top public courses in the country—instead of Crockery Hills. Sunday afternoon baseball changed to tennis. One of the few things that didn't change was our lively get-togethers at the family table. It was the same fun, the same debates, the same discussions—only the quantities changed. The boys ate big; Nancy, Laurie and I tried not to.

The regular golf season was better for Dan in his sophomore year. Thanks to an improved swing, he was medalist in eleven of sixteen matches. When he qualified for the state finals as an individual, I thought he had a very good chance to repeat as state champion. Unfortunately, on the tee of a par-3, he shanked three successive balls and took a nine on the hole. He finished sixteenth.

If you are a golfer, you are well aware that people who hit

shanks live in a lonely world. Other golfers treat the shanker as if he has leprosy. Other golfers don't like to be around a shanker or to even hear the word for fear that it might be an airborne contagion. On that one par-three, Dan caught the shanks. The first mutated into yet another, and then, unspeakably, into another. It's painful to watch, more painful to experience.

As his father, I was pleased that Dan accepted his performance with the good sportsmanship that golf is intended to foster.

Hockey also presented some problems for us that year. Jon went to Calvin College in Grand Rapids and soon became an impact player for that Division III program. Other kids that Dan played with headed for college as well, leaving a shortage of competition in Muskegon. We decided to explore the possibility of Dan playing travel hockey out of Grand Rapids. He would turn fifteen that year and several of the older boys he had been playing with growing up in Muskegon were playing for the Grand Rapids Amateur Hockey Association (GRAHA) Whalers, a midget team (fifteen–sixteen year olds) coached by Gordon Laxton, a former goalie with the Pittsburgh Penguins.

Nancy and I discussed the pros and cons. The pros were: Dan didn't have much competition left in Muskegon; this would be good competition that would push him to improve; he would have a coach that knew something about hockey instead of me; we could share rides with two boys from Muskegon that played on the team. The cons included: practices were in Grand Rapids two nights a week; games were in Detroit every weekend; there wouldn't be as much parental supervision as we would have liked.

The decision was not taken lightly and, in the end, it was a family decision. The overriding factor in the decision was: If Dan had any hope of playing college hockey, which he did, he had to keep progressing. Fortunately, he had demonstrated a high level of maturity for his age so we concluded that it wasn't a big risk. After a combined total of thirty-four years of successfully avoiding organized travel hockey our four boys—we decided to let our youngest do it.

We signed up to play Midgets but GRAHA officials noticed that Dan was technically a second-year Bantam. They insisted he play in his own age bracket—on the Bantam team. Now the ride sharing, playing with some of his old teammates, and learning from Gordon Laxton was all nullified. So . . . Dan attended practices for a short while and played one game with the Bantams, but he was not impressed. "If I have to play this level of hockey," he said, "I might as well save us a lot of grief and play in Muskegon."

Fortunately, Gordie Laxton's Midget team was short of players so he called us to find out why Dan decided not to play for him. He was irate after we explained the actions of the GRAHA officials. "You have Dan show up for practice with my Midget team on Tuesday," he told me, with *a lot* more color than I'm relating. "I'll handle the GRAHA officials."

Laxton was true to his word and it turned out to be great for Dan's development. Number one, he was two years younger than most of the sixteen-year-olds that made up the league so he was forced to step up his game. Number two, the team was short of players. Quite often only two lines dressed, which meant that Dan got to play half the time, versus playing on a team with a full complement of four lines and playing only twenty-five percent of the time. Number three, there were several feisty players on the team. When the Grand Rapids team would get ahead, the other team would send in their fourth line to instigate an altercation. These feisty players were only too happy to oblige. This meant they spent a lot of time in the penalty box and Dan got even more ice time. He led the team in scoring with 40 goals and 57 assists in 50 games.

It was not the best life experience for Dan, and it was very time-consuming for parents and players. Every other weekend or so, a parent would travel with the team to Detroit to act as a chaperone. Four people to a motel room and too many Big Macs and fries, while the other parent held down the fort back home was not my idea of how a family should function. It was problematic for Dan as well. Two hours of travel for a one-hour practice—twice a week. Then a tedious three-hour ride to Detroit for a two-hour game, hang around until the next day for another game, and then a three-hour ride back home.

Even before the season was over, we were concerned that Dan was approaching burnout. And he was still only fifteen years old.

Because of his play on the Midget team the previous year, Dan was invited to attend the Michigan Midget Sports Festival. The top sixty-eight hockey players with 1969 and 1970 birth dates would be assembled in Oak Park, MI, for a three day festival where they would play, as the letter of invitation stated, ". . . in front of a panel of college head coaches and professional scouts who will rate your performance throughout the festival. These ratings will be utilized for recommendations to the various American Hockey Association of the United States summer camps."

It would be a good opportunity to compare Dan's development with his peers so Nancy and I both went along to observe. Although he was one of the youngest participants, at 6' 2" and 180 pounds he was one of the biggest. After watching him compete, I also thought he was one of the best. Not the fanciest, not the most dazzling, but one of the best. Unfortunately, he wasn't one of those selected to participate in any of the advanced camps. It was disappointing. Like Nancy, I had to wonder if I knew what I was looking at, and whether I was afflicted with "father's eyes."

Apparently, Dan wasn't as good as we thought.

Not long after the Michigan Midget Sports Festival, I received a phone call from a man who identified himself as the owner and general manager of a Junior "B" team (seventeen–twenty year old players) in Canada. On the line with him was the coach of the team. The GM explained that Dan had been recommended to them by Bill (Wilkie) Wilkinson, the current head hockey coach at Western Michigan University and an assistant coach at Bowling Green when Scott played there. As we talked, it became clear that the GM was not offering Dan a tryout but an actual spot on the team. "If Wilkie says Dan will play Division I in a year or two," he said, "and Dan can play Junior 'B' *now*, that's good enough for us."

The two men described the city as an affluent community with excellent schools. The GM added that his teams usually finished first or second in the league and that his program was geared to produce scholarship players for Division I schools. He emphasized he ran a "family" program.

We were invited to visit the city, meet the executives of the team, some of the players, and see the hockey facilities and the school that Dan would be attending. At the same time we could also meet the family with whom Dan would be living. Before we hung up, the GM reiterated that they were not offering a tryout. Dan had a spot on the team if he wanted it. All living, educational, and hockey expenses would be paid for.

Needless to say, I was dumbfounded and full of questions. Dan wasn't good enough to make the Michigan Select Midget Team, but he *was* good enough to play for one of the best Junior 'B' teams in Canada? Without a tryout? Another question was whether he was ready to leave home; he was only fifteen. What had Bill Wilkinson seen that the Michigan Select Midget Team selection committee hadn't?

As a family involved in hockey, we always knew—if Dan wanted to play hockey in college—he might have to leave home in his senior year of high school and play Juniors in Canada or take grade thirteen in Canada after graduation from the twelfth grade at home. It was a route a lot of college hockey players took. But leave home for his junior year? I wasn't sure if Dan was ready for this, but I knew that Nancy and I were not.

After the whole family talked it over, we accepted the invitation and made the visit. We were impressed with the GM, his family, the coach, the executives that we met, the ice facility, the school, and the city. As Dan said on the ride home, "What's not to like? It's got everything we could ask for."

From the very beginning, we made it clear that this was to be Dan's decision. Whatever it was, we would support it. After giving it some thought, he told us he wanted to stay home for another year and think about Canada for his senior year. I didn't know if that was the right way to go or not, but it was his decision.

What I also didn't know was that he wasn't happy with it.

Late on a warm August night, two weeks after Dan had decided not to go to Canada, Nancy and I were in bed when we thought we heard someone crying. Listening at the open window, I could tell that the sobbing was coming from the backyard and that there was more than one person involved. I went downstairs, looked out the door and saw Scott and Dan out in the yard. They were hugging each other and both were crying.

Before I could reach them, Scott blubbered, "We're fine, Dad, just fine. Go back in the house."

"What do you mean, you're just fine," I said. "Obviously, something is drastically wrong."

"Nothing's wrong," Scott said. "Just go back in the house, okay? Please!"

I did as he asked. When I got back to the bedroom, Nancy came away from the window with a worried look. "What do you think is wrong?"

"I haven't a clue. But my guess is that it has something to do with Canada."

When the caterwauling was still going on an hour later, I called out to the boys and asked them if they were sure that everything was all right.

"We're fine," one of them sobbed. "Go back to bed."

Sure. I was supposed to just go to sleep while my oldest and youngest sons were blubbering to each other over who knew what.

When they finally cried out all the tears they had, they came up to our bedroom and confirmed my suspicions. "I've decided I have to go to Canada and give it a try," Dan said. "I couldn't sleep on the decision to stay home."

We drove to Canada late in August with Dan's equipment and enough clothes for two weeks—the length of the team's usual try-out period. Dan would live with the GM and his wife during that time. We stayed long enough to watch the Sunday evening practice. In size or speed, Dan did not look out of place. Leaving the practice and not knowing if he would be coming back home, made for a very long ride back to Grand Haven.

He phoned home on a regular basis. Things were going well. Yes, he thought he could play at this level. He missed home but everyone was being very good to him. Near the end of the two weeks, I phoned the GM to be certain that this had not been a mistake. "Should I come and pick him up," I asked, "or bring his winter clothes?"

He laughed. Was I kidding? Dan was a real find and they were thrilled to have him. He'll be playing in the NHL some day.

The NHL some day? I dismissed the comment as over-exuberance.

We took his clothes, his golf clubs, and some personal things to remind him of home to Canada. The GM indicated to me that in order for Dan to attend school and have medical coverage, it was necessary to assign legal guardianship of Dan to him. I thought it unusual, but I signed.

After visiting several times, we were pleased with the way that Dan was adapting to his new environment. On September 8, I wrote to the GM and his wife to express our appreciation for this opportunity for Dan. In part the letter read:

> *Since Dan was (as you say) "a wee one," we thought that God had given him special gifts and that one day we would lose him to some athletic pursuit or another. Yet when the decision and the "one day" came, it came as if we didn't expect it. And we, like he, had lumps in our throats, wondering if and hoping that this was the right thing for Dan.*
>
> *And then there was the wait to see if our expectations and Wilkie's assessments were too high and whether Dan was ready to break what we think are very strong family ties.*
>
> *As we drove home yesterday afternoon, we talked of many things, and one thing was certain . . . that we were entirely comfortable in leaving Dan in the charge of the likes of the two of you. You have been forthright, sincere, and honest from the first phone call, an approach that we very much appreciate. And you have opened your home and heart to Dan and us in a way that we didn't dare anticipate.*

We had no way of knowing how wrong we were.

All of Dan's reports were positive and he appeared to be doing very well. He scored the team's first goal of the season. By the end of October he had four goals and nine assists in ten games. The GM told us that universities such as Princeton, Dartmouth, R.P.I., Bowling Green and Western Michigan had expressed an interest in Dan.

During a visit in October, Dan took me aside just before we left for home and asked me to call him at exactly 4:10 on the following Monday afternoon. He had something he needed to talk to me about and he would be home alone at that time.

I called him from work at exactly 4:10 and I remember the conversation as if it were this morning.

"What's up, Dano?"

In as serious a tone as I ever heard from him, Danny said, "Dad, listen. I think (the GM) is hitting on me."

I didn't say anything for a few seconds, not wanting to acknowledge what I'd just heard. "He's *hitting* you?"

"No, Dad. Hitting *on* me."

"You mean . . .?"

"That's what I mean."

"Pack your stuff," I said. "We can be there in five-and-a-half hours."

"No, no, you can't do that," he said. "This guy *owns* me, and he can make it so I never play hockey in Canada again. You have to figure out a way to get me out of here without losing my playing card."

"But what about you?"

"I can deal with it for a few more days but not much longer than that," Dan said. "He's playing with my mind like you *can't* believe."

"Like what?"

"Like, 'How bad do you want to play college hockey?' And, 'What's it worth to you to play on this team?' He won't let me get any sleep."

"What do you mean by that?"

"He keeps me up until four in the morning, talking."

"Danny . . . has he gotten to you?"

"No," he said. "And I won't let him get close."

My mind was reeling and it felt inadequate telling him to hang in there. "We'll figure something out," I promised. "And we'll get you out of there as soon as possible."

"We have a game Tuesday," Danny said, "and it's worse after games. That's when he gets drunk and won't let me alone."

"I'll get back to you with a plan as soon as I can get something worked out," I said. "Try not to alert him that we're going to do something."

"I won't."

"Okay. Listen, we love you and we'll get you out of this mess. Are you sure you're all right?"

"I'm okay."

"Hang tough."

"I will."

We said goodbye to each other and hung up. It was a parent's worst nightmare come true.

Driving home from work, my emotions whipped around like ingredients in a blender. *Rage* . . . toward the GM for misappropriating our trust. *Guilt* . . . for allowing Dan to leave home in the first place. *Fear* . . . for what yet might happen to him before we could get him out of there. *Concern* . . . for Dan's well-being. *Stupid* . . . for not being perceptive enough to see through his "kindness" and "generosity." *Helpless* . . . for being 360 miles away and unable to hold your child in your arms. The result was a recipe for sickness. I was sick at heart and sick to my stomach. I hurried home as fast as I could.

After commiserating with Nancy about the guilt we felt for letting him out of our sight, we got through the next few hours and the next four days planning how we were going to extricate Dan. Our first call was to some old friends, the O'Briens, who lived in a city that was adjacent to where Dan was staying. Their son had played at Bowling Green with Scott. They were aghast and took it as personal affront that someone in that position would take advantage of the situation, but the fact that this was within hockey, the national pastime, enraged them. They agreed to call Dan, arrange to go to the Tuesday night game, and take Dan out afterward to reduce the time he had to spend in the GM's house. They also offered their home to us as a base of operations for whatever was needed to get Dan out of there.

The next call was to Bill Wilkinson. He had recommended this program to us so we felt he should be made aware of what was going on. Also, since he was Canadian, perhaps he could give us direction. He agreed to have lunch with us the next day.

Wilkie was as enraged as the O'Briens were. As it turned out, the father of one of his players was a partner in a prestigious law firm in Canada. He said he would call the lawyer and seek his counsel. Wilkie felt as bad about this as we did but we assured him that we didn't hold him responsible for the GM's actions.

There were three issues to deal with. We had signed legal custody of Dan to the GM so we needed to get that rescinded. The GM's team owned Dan's playing rights in Canada, evidenced by a document called a playing card, so we needed to get the GM to release these rights by signing over Dan's playing card. Lastly, while we worked discreetly to get Dan out of Canada, we had to avoid any appearance that it was because he was homesick. It was a big issue with college coaches who were looking for players.

After engaging the services of J. Brett Ledger, an attorney with Osler, Hoskin & Harcourt, a large Toronto firm, we developed a plan. We would arrange to pick Dan up as he walked to school on Friday morning, take his books to school and leave them in his locker. We would then go back to the GM's house and pack up Dan's stuff. The O'Briens agreed to go along to assist and serve as witnesses to the fact that we only took Dan's belongings. Then we would confront the GM.

After spending an eternal night at the O'Briens, we left to pick up Dan. As we traced his route to the school, we spotted him walking alone. Emotion had piled up on top of consternation for the past five frantic days and sleepless nights. To finally see him was the beginning of the end of our nightmare and we began to feel some relief. I could not swallow the tightness in my throat or hold back the tears. We had him back. There were hugs and kisses and more tears. I'm sure he felt smothered; I hope he felt mothered and fathered as well.

Once we got Dan's things out of the house we met with the attorney, who questioned Dan as to what had exactly happened. Dan's body shook as he recounted the various incidents. Ledger concluded that under Canadian law this could be prosecuted as an assault. The attorney and I then went to a pre-arranged meeting with the GM. I had called and told him that a Major Junior 'A' scout (the highest level of amateur hockey) had contacted me regarding Dan and I didn't want to meet with the scout "without the benefit of his vast experience." He was pleased to have been consulted on a matter of such importance and had agreed to meet.

When we were comfortably settled in his large office, I came right to the point.

"I have deceived you," I said. "This is not a Major Junior 'A' scout. He's an attorney that I engaged after Dan told me what has been going on after hours in your home. He's here to handle the legal issues and to make sure I don't lose control and come over your desk and strangle you. Perhaps it goes without saying, but your use of your position and relationship to engage in this kind of behavior disgusts me beyond words. I have no intention of making trouble for you," I told him. "I am only interested in securing the recession of your legal guardianship, getting Dan's playing card and his equipment, and getting him out of Canada as fast as we can. Again, I have no intention of making trouble for you. I only want to extract Dan from the sphere of your influence."

The color had drained from the GM's face. He looked like a cornered rat. In his nervousness or shock at being confronted, he accidentally bumped his toupee out of place and he became a pathetic sight. At one point, he stammered something about the boy misinterpreting his genuine affection for him.

The GM signed the release that the attorney had prepared and assured us that he would release Dan's playing card without delay. After I read—and he verbally approved—the press release I had written, we got Dan's hockey gear from the arena and left the city.

Two other Junior "B" programs—Stratford and St. Marys–had earlier expressed an interest in Dan. St. Marys had an immediate opening.

On the way back to Michigan, we stopped at Stratford so that Dan could see the ice rink and meet the executives. We then drove to St. Marys and got there in time for the Friday night game. After watching one period, Dan said, "Let's get out of here and get me home."

Once back in Michigan, I felt that Dan's playing hockey in Canada was over for the year. I told him to take the week off from school and collect himself. On Monday morning, though, he called me at work and asked to meet for lunch. While we ate, he said he knew he had to go back. His choice was St. Marys. He asked me to make the arrangements and find out if he could play in the game coming up that Friday.

I was pleased. To me, it meant that he had faced his demon and he knew who it was, and who it was not. It was not him, not hockey, not sports, and not Canada.

I phoned Scott Graham, the coach of the Lincolns, and told him that Dan would accept his invitation to play on their team and that we would be there in time for the game on Friday. Graham was pleased. He promised that everyone in St. Marys would do whatever they could to see that Dan's experience was the best it could be.

We arrived at St. Marys in plenty of time for Dan to get ready for the game and to meet his new teammates. After he warmed-up with the team, we learned that he couldn't play because the GM from the previous team was withholding his player card for C$1,000 in compensation. One week later—after a threatening letter from our lawyer, a call from me to the president of the Ontario Hockey League, and a payment of C$600 in compensation from the Lincolns—St. Marys finally secured Dan's release from his previous team.

I don't know how to label Dan's experience. Had Dan misinterpreted the questionable behavior of someone who had too much to drink? I do know that when I heard of how Sheldon Kennedy endured years of mental and sexual abuse from his Junior coach, I wondered how close my own son came to the same horror. I want the point of this part of our story to be unmistakably clear. It is not to reveal there is questionable behavior in hockey; there is questionable behavior in life. Sports are a microcosm of life and hockey is a microcosm of sports. The point is that, as parents, our mission is to instill our children with moral fiber, self esteem, street smarts, and a trust in their parents so if bizarre behavior is encountered, the child will recognize it. The child must know that when things get so bad he cannot deal with them alone, he can rely on the safety net of his family.

There is also a lesson here for league officials, executives, and coaches—all of the adults who have positions of responsibility in youth hockey or organized youth sports at any level. Abuse and harassment—psychological, physical, and sexual—happen; they have been widely publicized in the recent past and some of the damage has been horrific and permanent. We must continue to be on the lookout for such situations, because to pretend that sports are somehow immune from evil or deviant behavior is to allow it to happen. The recommendations made through Gordon Kirke's "Players First," a report commissioned by the Canadian Hockey League, should have the active support of officials and parents alike in all of amateur sports.

A great deal of one's preparation for the NHL has nothing to do with hockey.

St. Marys did everything they promised to make Dan's experience very positive. The Parkinson family, who already had one player staying with them, Scott Garrow, agreed to take Dan in as well. Ken Malvern, the principal of the high school (St. Marys District Collegiate & Vocational Institute) was also happy to have Dan. He welcomed, as he put it, all "hockey players who were serious students." The team seemed to accept Dan, too, especially Coach Graham and General Manager Angelo "Angie" Nigro, a short, barrel-chested man with a raspy voice.

Angie (who sounded like Anthony Quinn doing a Marlon Brando impression) had once been a trainer with the Buffalo Sabres. "That young Bylsma lad there," he would growl, "he's gonna be a keeper, that one. You don't notice him until you look at the score sheet and see his name poppin' up week after week. Eh?"

There were two players on the St. Marys Lincolns that Dan

would meet again in the NHL—Bob Boughner, who became a defenseman for the Buffalo Sabres, and Scott Driscoll, who became a linesman.

Dan had a good year with the Lincolns. He scored 14 goals and had 28 assists in 27 games. More important than the stats, he began to get recruiting letters from college coaches and attention from NHL scouts.

Because he was only a second year Midget, he was eligible for the Canadian Junior "A" draft that summer. I learned from Angie that "your lad is ranked right up in the Central Scouting rankings there." Actually, he was ranked 20th. It meant that Dan was considered to be among the top twenty Midget players in all of the U.S. and Canada.

Dick Todd (currently an assistant coach of the New York Rangers) at that time was the General Manager of the Peterborough Petes, a top Junior 'A' program. Todd had contacted Dan on several occasions recruiting him to play for the Petes (a coveted option if Dan was not going to college). He indicated the Petes would select Dan in the first round of the draft if he would commit to playing Junior 'A' instead of going to college. Todd also mentioned things like "potential for the NHL soon." Dan declined, saying he wanted to play in college. The Petes drafted him anyway but didn't waste a first round pick.

Todd was a respected GM in Canadian junior hockey. Did he mean it when he said that Dan had the potential to play in the NHL or was that recruiting hype? Still, he was willing to commit a first round pick.

Danny, Danny. What will become of you?

When the hockey season finished in early March, Dan returned home and resumed high school at West Michigan Christian High in time to begin baseball. During his junior season, he began to hit for power which showed in his statistics. He had 24 hits in 57 at bats, including eleven doubles ("Gibby shots") and two home runs, for a .412 batting average. He also stole 25 bases in 26 attempts. We still went to Sluka Field after regular practice and I hit balls to him until my hands were raw. He was named to the All-Conference, All-District, All-Regional, and the All-Muskegon area first teams.

Summer was filled with a job mowing lawns for a commercial landscape maintenance service, Dykstra Landscaping. Jim Dykstra had moved to Grand Haven from Chicago at the same time we moved back from Orland Park. For the most part, the boys worked summers for Jim until they got their jobs after college. Dan has worked all or parts of eleven summers mowing lawns and spreading wood chips for Jim. The boys have all been inducted into the mythical Dykstra Landscaping Hall of Fame.

These were great summer jobs. There's nothing like monotonous manual labor to whet a person's appetite for the return of the school year and attacking one's studies with a renewed sense of purpose. Dykstra has often claimed his business wouldn't have survived without the Bylsma boys, but when accounts are all settled, I know I will still owe Jim Dykstra.

That same summer, Dan was invited back to the Michigan Midget Sports Festival. As usual, I had hopes that Dan would be selected to attend the National Midget Sports Festival. My reasoning was simple. The Michigan camp would be attended by players who had been playing at the Midget level; that is fifteen- and sixteen-year-olds. Dan had been competing successfully in Canadian Junior 'B'; that is, seventeen- to twenty-year-olds. He was ranked in the top twenty of all sixteen-year-old hockey players in North America by Central Scouting, and was considered worthy of a first round pick by the Peterborough Petes. I expected him to be a standout player at the Michigan Midget Sports Festival.

When we arrived at the festival, I wandered over to an observation window overlooking the rink while Dan checked in. Two men were standing at the window talking. I recognized one from the year before as Don Burton, the director of the festival. I assumed the other man was the father of one of the participants.

The conversation that I overheard went something like this:

Father: "So, do you have a pretty good idea of who's going to Colorado Springs?"

Burton: "Yeah, we pretty much know. We've been watching

these kids for a few years now. Unless someone comes in here and blows our socks off, it's pretty much set."

Came the dawn! For two years now, Dan had been coming to these sports festivals as a tackling dummy. Or was I the dummy? I recalled what Nancy had said after the Bantam Camp, "I thought he was one of the best kids on the ice, but I don't always know what I'm looking at." And I remembered my reaction to how I ranked Dan at the previous year's Midget camp, "Not the fanciest, not the most dazzling, but one of the best."

I told Nancy what I suspected. After debating a bit, we decided we should tell Dan what I had heard. When I finished the story, I said, "If you have an idea that you would like to go to Colorado Springs, you're going to have to 'knock their socks off.'"

Of the thirty-six forwards who attended the festival, there were five besides Dan who had played Juniors the year before. Admittedly, I could only watch the festival with a father's eyes. But I thought he *was* 'blowing their socks off.' Only one forward was bigger than Dan's 6' 2" and 190 pound frame, and Dan used his size to dominate. He had seven goals and two assists in three games and was the leading scorer in the festival.

It was disappointing when he found out he had not been selected to go to Colorado Springs. When Bill Wilkinson heard that Dan had not be chosen, he was incredulous. "I can't believe they passed over him," he said. "You tell Dan these selections don't mean anything; they're just flowers."

Perhaps it was just flowers, but everyone likes to get flowers. It didn't seem fair. But then, not everything in sports—or life—is fair. Even though I had been giving that advice to my children for years, it was a bitter pill to swallow when I saw it happen again to Dan.

I was pleased when I saw that the selection fiasco didn't sour him or diminish his love for sports, hockey in particular. It was yet another reminder of the importance of preparing your child for the vagaries of life. I wish I knew then what I know now about other kids with great talent who have been passed over just like he was. I would have told Dan that great NHL players like Bill Guerin, Tony Amonte, and John LeClair were passed over and never played on the amateur USA Olympic Teams.

As the school year approached, Dan seemed anxious to get back to St. Marys. He had developed good friends on the team and at school and was confident of his role with the Lincolns. Dan had a singular focus: become good enough to earn a hockey scholarship from a Division I university. He wanted to "get on with it."

For the upcoming year, he was to live with Nelson and Heather Goad. He was a welcomed guest in the homes of several other families as well. The trip to St. Marys became a social affair for us as well as a chance to see Dan. There was brunch at the Stephens's (the family of a classmate friend) or a trip to see Steve Coultes's (the team's goalie) family's beef cattle operation or pizza with this family or that after the games.

As the season progressed, Dan received calls and more recruiting letters from a large number of schools. To stop some of the calls and letters, he let it be known that he was only interested in offers from colleges in the Central Collegiate Hockey Association (CCHA) so that he could play close to home, and his family could come to watch.

Dan had another good year. With 38 goals and 57 assists in 48 games, he was the leading scorer for the Lincolns and was the fourth leading scorer in the Western Conference. He also was selected to play in the Conference East-West All-Star game.

As the time to make a commitment drew near, Dan narrowed the schools he would consider attending to three: Bowling Green State University (B.G.), because his brother Scott played there and the coach, Jerry York, promised him he could wear Scott's #21; the University of Michigan, because I graduated from there and because of its outstanding academics; and Western Michigan University, because of his friendship with head coach Bill Wilkinson.

In the end, the choice was Bowling Green and the opportunity to wear Scott's old number. On April 13, 1988, Dan signed the coveted National Letter of Intent to accept a full scholarship to attend B.G. The signing occurred after Nancy had prepared a sumptuous prime rib dinner to celebrate the occasion and to entertain the coaches from B.G. It was a satisfying moment, and we didn't think of the terrible GM incident all evening.

There are a couple of instances that stand out in my mind from

Dan's senior year at St. Marys. During a phone call, he related to me that he was playing on the varsity basketball team. "You?" I asked. "You haven't played basketball since the eighth grade."

"Yes, I know," he said. "But up here, an American kid is expected to be able to play basketball like we think all Canadian kids play hockey. Several of the hockey players are on the team. We practice and play during seventh hour study hall so it doesn't interfere with hockey."

On a Friday evening sometime later, the photographer from the local newspaper, Pat Payton, came over to me during the hockey game and handed me a copy of the latest edition. "The Yank has done it again," he said, smiling. "This time in basketball."

An article in the sports section (including five photos) reported that the St. Marys Salukis had beaten the previously undefeated Stratford Central Rams for the first time in the history of the schools' rivalry. A caption under a photo of Dan shooting a free throw read:

BYLSMA SINKS WINNING POINTS. Dan Bylsma of the senior Salukis coolly sank two free throws with 25 seconds remaining to play last Thursday against Stratford Central. The points stood up as the margin of victory as the Salukis stunned the Rams 61–59. Bylsma was the heart and soul of the St. Marys attack. The big forward fired a game-high 20 points.

And there was this in an accompanying article:

. . . (Salukis coach) Hunter claimed that Bylsma was 'by far the most valuable player on the court.'

Four years later Pat Payton called the game to mind during a visit he made to the States to cover college hockey. "I cover a lot of sports in my job," he told me, "and I have never before nor since experienced anything like what Dan did during that basketball game. He had a steely look in his eye you could see and an intensity that you could feel. He owned that game. He out-rebounded guys that were four inches taller than he; he canned shots from outside and inside. He played like one possessed.

"In a hockey game, he plays behind a mask and in an enclosed arena, so you don't always get a feel for the intensity. But if he plays hockey the same way, he'll go a long way."

He had often been called "Mr. Icicle Veins." Now he was the "heart and soul" of a basketball team. I had seen that intensity on the golf course, on the baseball diamond, in hockey rinks, even during our competition in the backyard. He had the ability to focus on the task at hand with such singular purpose that his intensity is palpable. It is something to experience.

Another notable experience came after the hockey season was over and Dan had returned home. The Lincolns were having an awards dinner at which he would be receiving an award as the leading scorer. Could we go? Absolutely.

On the way to St. Marys he indicated that the team would probably auction off the teams' jerseys as a way of raising funds. If it was possible, he said, he would like to have his jersey as a souvenir of his playing days for the Lincolns. He thought the jerseys would go for about C$25 to C$30.

At the auction that was held after the dinner and awards, the first few jerseys went for C$25 to C$35. One of the more popular player's jerseys went for C$75 and another went for C$125. Number 21—Dan's—was the last one on the block. The moment I bid C$30, someone else bid C$50. The bidding went up in C$50 increments in the blink of an eye or two. When I bid on it at C$300, the auctioneer quickly shouted, "Sold!" He had cut the bidding off in my favor, for which I was a lot grateful and a little embarrassed.

Later, I went to Joe Taylor, one of the two men who were also bidding on Dan's jersey. He was the owner of the local Ford/Lincoln/Mercury dealership and his dealership's name was on the back of Dan's jersey as a sponsor.

"Why did you have such an interest in Dan's jersey?" I asked.

"I would have paid a thousand dollars for that jersey," he replied. "That kid's going to be in the NHL someday."

Dan's going to be in the NHL someday? Yes, and pigs have

wings. Yet it was the third time I'd heard similar comments. First Dan's former GM, Dick Todd, and now Joe Taylor.

Danny, Danny. What will become of you?

With hockey season over, Dan could concentrate on baseball and graduating from West Michigan Christian High. One of the differences in the discipline between Canadian and American education was exemplified at our first parent-teacher conference after Dan was back at W.M.C.H.

At each conference, we always asked the same question, "Is he respectful, kind, diligent, trustworthy, etc.? In short, does he conduct himself as a gentleman?"

When we asked it this time, the teacher hesitated for a telling moment before saying, "Dan has been showing some disrespect since he's been back."

I was surprised. Mild-mannered Dan? The Dan that I could punish with a harsh look? "Really? How does he show this disrespect?"

"Whenever I call on him," the teacher said, "he addresses me as 'Sir.' The women teachers have reported that he calls them 'Ma'am.'"

Nancy and I looked at each other and began to laugh. "In Canada," I explained to the teacher, "a student is expected to address his teacher formally. You may not answer 'Yes,' you must say 'Yes, Sir.' He answers us that way sometimes."

Amazing. Simply because he used a formal form of address, he was misunderstood as being disrespectful. It caused me to wonder how far the U.S. educational system had come and in what direction?

Dan was to exceed all expectations in his senior year in baseball. The coaches, Joe Hicks and Sam DeBoer, surmised that I had something to do with Dan's hitting skills. Because of that, and because Joe's health was failing, I was invited to be an assistant coach. I worked with the kids on their hitting and was the third base coach; Sam handled defense and pitching and was the first base coach. Joe remained in the dugout and masterminded the attack. I quickly accepted, so that I could be a part of Dan's senior season.

While his bat was his strength, Dan could beat you with his base-stealing, his fielding, and his leadership. Joe, Sam, and I were glad we were coaching on Dan's side of the field. He finished the year with 30 hits, including 8 home runs, in 59 at-bats for an average of .509. He stole 26 bases in 26 attempts, knocked in 33 runs, and scored 34 times himself. He made All-Everything, including All-State, and was selected as an outfielder on the Dream Team—the best player at each position in all classes in Michigan high school baseball. He also played in Tiger Stadium in the Michigan High School Coaches' All-Star game in Detroit. Appropriately, he started in right field . . . on the very same grass that his hero, Kirk Gibson, once roamed.

Throughout that season, after almost every team practice, the two of us still went to Sluka Field and did the fly ball thing.

It had been a spectacular high school baseball career. He had a four-year batting average of .425, had scored or driven in four runs for every five official times at bat, and he stole 84 bases out of 85 attempts.

Many people said, "God sure blessed that kid with incredible talent!" Yes, He did. But more importantly, God blessed that kid with an incredible work ethic. Dan worked hard to get as good as he was and he kept working hard to get better. Then he worked some more. He was a kid who knew how to compete and loved the challenge of competition—in-your-face competition.

Let *me* bat.

Go ahead, try to throw it past me.

I *dare* you to try and hit over my head.

I'm going to steal on the next pitch. I *challenge* you to try and throw me out.

You think you can score from second on a single to center field? Try it.

Play me deep. I'll bunt.

If you walk me, I'll be at second base on the next pitch. Third on the next.

I'll *find* a way to beat you.

All of it was silently said with steely eyes. And all of it was with an intense focus. Until, that is, the game was over. Then that pumpkin-face grin would come out and the Gibby poster would come down.

Until the next time he "laced 'em up."

Because of his outstanding season with the Lincolns and on the recommendation of B.G.'s head coach, Jerry York, Dan was selected to attend the 1988 U.S. National Junior Camp. Thirty-seven players assembled at Lake Placid for a one-week tryout for the 1988–89 National Junior Team. The names of the other forwards didn't mean anything to me at the time, but some of them were to become very familiar stars in the NHL: Tony Amonte, Ted Donato, John LeClair, Shawn McEachern, Jeremy Roenick, and Joe Sacco, among others. Of the twenty-one forwards in the camp, twelve or thirteen made the National Junior Team but Dan wasn't one of them. He simply did not have a good camp and appeared, to me, tentative. It was as if he lacked confidence.

He indicated later that most of the other guys knew each other from the Select 16 and Select 17 Camps but he was an unknown, an outsider. He felt as if he didn't fit in and it made him uncomfortable. It showed in his play.

On the drive from Lake Placid, I wondered how the National Junior Camp might have gone if . . . he had felt comfortable . . . if . . . he had not been passed over at the Michigan Midget Camps . . . if . . . life were only fair. But then, " . . . if ifs and ands were pots and pans, beggars would ride horses."

We drove straight to Bowling Green, Ohio, and dropped him off at college to continue his education, play Division I ice hockey, and try out for the baseball team.

DAN

High school started earlier than originally expected. I had the option of starting at West Michigan Christian High (W.M.C.H.) in the ninth grade instead of finishing my ninth grade year at my elementary school. I thought I might be ready for high school sports, but didn't like the idea of going to a new school with few friends. But being fearful of meeting new classmates and making new friends did not overcome my desire to play sports in high school. In the fall, I found myself at W.M.C.H.

Sports helped me get acclimated to my new surroundings and soon I assumed the #2 spot behind Jon on the golf team. I was not on my game and had trouble beating him. In private, I enjoyed beating any of my brothers in any sport. But being the #2 golfer to my high school senior brother was comfortable. I struggled most of the season but with some help from Jon and some unexpected outstanding rounds from our team-mates, we advanced to the state tournament.

What happened that fall day is something I've never really been able to understand. Winning the state tournament is something that had won bragging rights for my oldest brother Scott, and something I wanted desperately to win as well. That Saturday, I hit the ball very average and not a single part of my game was particularly on fire. Through the first nine holes, I scrambled to shoot a 38 which put me two back of the leader. I thought that a 36 on the back nine and the resulting 74 was probably what I needed to win.

After a missed birdie opportunity at the 10th hole, I began to build some momentum by making a long par putt on the 11th. After four solid pars on 12, 13, 14, and 15, I scrambled to make another par on the 16th. When I rolled in a long birdie putt on the par-5 17th, I felt I might be closing in on the leaders. But then a poor drive on 18 left me with a shot over trees and a bunker to a pin tucked very close to the edge of the sand. I didn't want to lose by one stroke, and I thought I needed a birdie to ensure at least a tie. I probably should have pitched up to the front of the green, but laying up—that is, playing it safe—had never been in my lesson plan. You never laid up when you were trying to win one of the tournaments in the backyard.

Fortunately, I got the shot up quickly enough to clear the trees in my line and it landed just over the bunker and stopped within a few feet of the pin. I made the putt for another birdie to go to even par for the day and became the State Champion. That shot and making the putt for a birdie are fuzzy memories, but jumping into my brother Jon's arms just off the green is a memory that sticks with me to this day.

In the spring, the baseball team started workouts and I was busy trying to figure out which position would provide me with the most playing time. The regular third baseman had graduated so it looked like third base might give me the opportunity I needed to start or at least get some playing time. I didn't tell the coach, Joe Hicks, that I had never played third. Even though I thought that I deserved to be in the starting lineup on opening day, the coach informed the freshmen that we had to earn a spot over the older players.

I was steamed. There was no question, in *my* mind anyhow, that I could hit better than three or four of the players that were starting. It wasn't fair. My father's advice was the same as always: "Life isn't fair. Work hard and be ready for your chance. It will come, trust me."

After watching from the dugout for a couple of games and pinch-hitting on occasion, I decided that I might be able to steal the starting position in left field. With that in mind, I begged my father to go to Sluka Field and hit fly balls to me. He did it until he insisted his hands were sore and we had to go home. To me it wasn't hard work, it was a game. And since I wasn't playing much for the team, I created my own game at Sluka Field.

Every fly ball Dad hit to me was a different situation against a different team. I knew I would get an opportunity and I wanted to be prepared. Growing up as the youngest of four boys taught me that it was your actions on the field that gained respect, not your age. Being a freshman meant I had to do things better and work harder, and I believed that if I worked hard enough and proved I was capable, being a freshman wouldn't matter.

I got some timely hits as a pinch-hitter and by the fifth or sixth game, I started in left field. Fortunately, I played well enough to keep my starting job for the rest of the season. As the state tournament rolled around, the Warriors (8–10 on the year) weren't expected to do much of anything. But winning streaks take on a life of their own: each win builds on the last. Teams and players get on rolls that build into something exciting. The team rallied around my poster of Detroit Tiger star Kirk Gibson and we started to play with an attitude that we weren't going to be beat.

The backyard taught me that the best thing about sports was challenging your opponents (brothers) one-on-one and coming out on top. I was fortunate to get some of those opportunities that baseball season. I remember sitting in the dugout hoping that the game would come down to me and my turn at bat.

My dad was right again. "Be ready, be prepared. Your chance will come." I was. It did. I was fortunate enough to be an important part of winning a state high school championship in baseball. Heady stuff for a fourteen-year-old freshman.

As the 1985–86 hockey season approached, we learned that two of my friends who were among the best players from Muskegon were planning on playing hockey for the Grand Rapids Whalers' AAA Major Midget team. I thought it might be a cool idea to play on the Whalers with them. My parents weren't so sure. After all, these other players were sixteen years old and I was fourteen. I argued in favor of joining my friends. They were going to play in Grand Rapids, why couldn't I? I was the same caliber player. Playing more games and against better teams seemed like a good thing. While Mom and Dad still weren't certain of the value of this step, I ended up playing for the Grand Rapids team.

Everything I anticipated turned out to be true. The number of games and the talent of the teams the Whalers played against forced me to advance my game to levels beyond what I would have accomplished if I had continued playing in Muskegon. But my parents' apprehension turned out to be well-founded in a way they were wise enough to foresee but I wasn't.

Traveling twice a week to practice in Grand Rapids (an hour's drive each way) proved difficult for everybody. But it was playing two games after a tedious three-hour drive to Detroit and then three tiresome hours back every weekend that began to suck the fun out of the game.

Almost all our games were road games because the Detroit teams refused to come to Grand Rapids to play. By the end of the season, I wasn't sure I wanted to play hockey anymore—ever. Had I been the one who wanted to do this? Were my parents pushing me, pressuring me to do what *they* thought I should do? The only thing I knew for sure was that I wanted baseball to start as soon as possible.

I was invited to several select hockey camps over the course of my high school years. These invitations came with hopes of being selected to move on to a U.S.A national team. Each occasion yielded the same unsatisfactory results; after the camp was over, I received the same form letter, "Thanks for coming, but you didn't fit into the Select Team's plans." I didn't think I could claim that I was the best player at any of the camps, but based on the performances of the other kids, I felt that I should have been in the running for a spot on the Select Team.

With each camp, my disappointment over not being selected grew, and my father's explanations never came close to placating my frustration. Each disappointment was another lesson in "Life's not always fair" and "Work hard, do your best, your chance will come."

Those words of wisdom make sense now, but back then . . .

I learned of the call from Canada while I was returning from a golf tournament in Mt. Pleasant, Michigan. My mother had stopped to call home to let my dad know how I had done and the time we could be expected to arrive home. It was then that Dad dropped the bomb on us. "Dan's been invited to play for a Junior 'B' team in Canada."

My first reaction to the invitation was elation. This was cool. Somehow this meant that whoever made the selections for the Select Camp had been wrong! Canada, the birthplace of hockey. The land of Wayne Gretzky and the Montreal Canadiens. The Junior 'B' League was the most advanced level of hockey I could play and retain eligibility for college. I had to pinch myself repeatedly to make sure I wasn't dreaming.

But soon I began to realize that accepting the invitation would change my life forever. It meant leaving home and going to a new home and school, leaving my friends and girlfriend behind. No more sports other than hockey. No more homecoming, school dances, or prom.

Was it worth it? Giving up my normal life to make a new one—just for hockey? Is hockey what I wanted to do? I wasn't that excited about hockey anyway . . . was I? Maybe I wanted to play baseball, maybe golf. I decided to decline the offer and stay home, but it wasn't long before I started second-guessing my decision

I had a heightened awareness of things around me as if life had become a serious matter at age fifteen. The words of familiar songs heard on the radio started to take on new meanings. Television shows suddenly were addressing some of the issues I was dealing with. At church, a sermon on the obligations to use one's talents could not have been directed at anyone but me. I struggled with my decision, knowing deep down that it was as unsettled as my stomach. But staying home with friends and family was an easier choice and a lot less scary.

Late one night, I confided to my oldest brother Scott that I was struggling with whether my decision to decline the Canadian offer was the right one. We went into the backyard, the same backyard where I had battled my brothers in the carefree pursuits of childhood competition, now to battle my demons. I told him that even though Mom and Dad had made it clear that the decision was mine to make and they accepted my decision not to go, I felt enormous pressures to change the decision and accept the offer. I said that Mom and Dad weren't pressuring me, but my whole life they had pressured me to be the best I could be and to do the right thing. I knew that the right thing to do—to be the best that I could be—was to go to Canada. But I didn't want to leave my home, my family, my friends, my high school. Not at age fifteen.

I told Scott I knew that his role on B.G.'s hockey team was limited until he was a senior because he hadn't gone to Canada to play. Now I was saying "no" to the opportunity Scott never had. I felt that I had developed the ability to play at an advanced level and that ability came with a corresponding, perhaps sacred, responsibility. It might be called my karma, or fate, or that it was in the stars . . . whatever description you're comfortable with. But I wasn't comfortable. I had a troubled soul. That night, I poured it out to Scott.

We paced back and forth over the scene of our competitions. We explored every possible situation. Tears came unabashedly but didn't bring us any closer to deciding my future. Scott finally ended the session in the early morning by pointing to the sky. "Only two people can decide what is right for Dan Bylsma. You and God. Not me, not Mom or Dad, not your girlfriend, nobody else. Just you and God, and only you have to live with that decision."

I knew what the right decision was. Ever since I had said, "No," I had heard God's "Yes" in people's voices and in various songs. I knew Scott was right—in the end the decision had to be my own and no one else's. It was my dream, no one else's. And my dream was to get a full-ride scholarship to play collegiate hockey.

Little did I know how important it would become that the choice to attend school and play hockey in Canada was *my* decision and *my* dream, not something someone else decided for me or someone else's dream that I was living out.

Our first day in Canada, my parents and I met the man who was very clearly in charge of the team: the General Manager. He was a tall, middle-aged man with a very noticeable hairpiece that was professionally woven into what real hair he had left. For some reason, it contributed to my feeling that this was not a man you wanted to get on the wrong side of. He was the person to whom everybody answered, including the coach. He also seemed to have just the right things to say to the young men whose futures hung in the balance of his decisions.

The GM pointed out all the places and things that I needed to know about if I were to make the team; the team's home rink and dressing room, the school that I would be attending, and all the benefits the players on the team could expect once they made the team. It was enough to convince me that this really was what I wanted, though I still felt somewhat uncomfortable.

It was unsettling walking into the rink on the first day of tryouts. I was 360 miles and light years away from the L.C. Walker Arena where I played as a little boy and still I felt like a little boy. I guess I was. I was a fifteen-year-old registering with guys who could actually grow facial hair, players who could be playing in a men's league. When the actual tryouts got underway, however, and although there was strong competition, I felt I played as well as some of the players on last year's team. But then, I had been to tryouts before and being "as good as" had meant I would be going home. Even though my dad had been assured that I had a spot on the team, I was less confident. As tryouts progressed it became clear that I would be good enough to at least make the first couple of cuts.

But by no means had I started to settle in. I was being introduced to the guys who might be my new teammates and possible places I might stay if I made the team. My parents and I scouted out the school that I might be attending, and we were being escorted around a new city—a new country for that matter.

This was North America but it was also different. People went "aboot" their business. I was reprimanded for not spelling "color" the Canadian way—"colour." The last letter in the alphabet became "zed." And I was a "hawkie" player. One hundred and one reminders that this wasn't home. I had a scared feeling fluttering around in my stomach, a feeling that stuck with me each day and was still there when I awakened the next morning. I kept telling myself that it would go away. I surely hoped it would.

As tryouts proceeded, I started to feel that this might just work. But, just when I thought that making the team was coming down to me and a few other players, that hole-in-my-stomach feeling came rushing back. My parents decided that it was time to return home, without me. I remember the tears in my mother's eyes as she hugged me and disappeared into the family van. My father's handshake and hug were not enough to dispel the discomfort that manifested itself in the pit of my gut.

The GM had invited me to stay with his family at least until the team was picked. It was becoming clear that I was probably going to make the team. I was playing in the exhibition games and performing well, and members from last year's team were starting to include me in the social atmosphere. I knew this was the start of the road to college hockey. Playing in Canada for two years and performing well would almost guarantee me a spot on some Division I squad. My dream—of playing college hockey—was starting to take shape and it all would start with making this team. This was make or break.

One humid August evening late in the tryout camp, I went out for a run to keep my conditioning up even though I had a slight "charley horse." When I came up the driveway, the GM, who was sitting outside the front door with a drink in his hand, asked me to sit down. Winded from the run, I gladly slumped into the other chair across from him. We started talking about the team and how we had played in the exhibition games and how only a few more players needed to be cut before the start of the season. The GM started to ask more serious questions about me and my future.

How much did it mean to me to be a part of this team? What was I willing to do to make this team? How hard would I work if I did make the team? How serious was the charley horse in my thigh? What was I willing to give up in order to make the team? Would it be all right if I had to miss church once in a while? (My parents had stressed that it was their wish I go to church on Sundays.)

Up to that point, the questions didn't seem to be anything out of the ordinary for someone who was making a decision about the last few cuts on his hockey team. Our conversation was uninterrupted except for when he got up to get another drink, which was usually right after he finished the previous one. After a while, he said he wanted to continue the discussion down in his den. As the conversation wore on, the effects of his considerable consumption became more and more obvious. It also was clear that some of the questions he asked were starting to get a little bizarre.

He talked about how he had worked with many young adults at leadership retreats. He confided that he knew what young adults talked about and that it was okay to talk to him about those same things. He also informed me that in college he minored in athletic training and he was interested in exactly how my charley horse felt. He examined my leg with my sweat pants still on.

The questioning and his drinking continued. I answered the questions the best I could, not knowing what he was trying to get out of me. Was he testing me some how? If I answered the questions incorrectly, would I endanger my chances of making the team and thus playing college hockey?

I started to get a strange feeling when the GM inquired about my leg a second time and asked to look at it again. But I said okay. After all, he was concerned about my ability to play and he told me he was an athletic trainer . . . sort of.

I started to get nervous when the questions became a little more personal. Mixed in with, "What would you be willing to do to make the team?" and "What is it worth to me to take you to church?" were questions that no one had ever talked to me about. "Had I ever had a wet dream? How often? When was the first time I had ever masturbated? How many times a week did I masturbate?"

I didn't know how to answer. He insisted that I could tell him, because he had spent a lot of time with young adults and he already knew the answers. He said that he had been on retreats where they sat around campfires and talked about this stuff. "So, when was the first time you masturbated? What is it worth to you to make this hockey team? How often do you masturbate? What are you willing to give up in order to make this hockey team? Do you still have wet dreams?" I was terrified. I felt he was trying to back me down and didn't really know what was going on, but I knew I couldn't give in.

The conversation returned to my charley horse. He explained how the muscles in the leg were attached to the muscles in the stomach through the groin. He expressed concern that the problem with my leg was not just in my leg but possibly a leg/groin/stomach problem. He asked to see my leg again, this time with my sweat pants down. He touched my leg where the charley horse was and asked me to move it up and down and also to flex my leg muscles. When the examination was over, the GM retreated for yet another drink.

All I wanted was to be able to go to my bedroom and hide behind the door, but I knew I couldn't leave that basement den. This just wasn't right, and it was close to 2:30 a.m. I hadn't made the team yet and the man who held my fate in his hands was testing me—why?

When he returned, he continued the grilling. The same questions over and over. "I'll take myself to church" wasn't a good enough answer. How was I supposed to answer "What was it worth to me to play on this team?" and "What was I willing to do to make the team?" It wasn't enough to explain that I would do just about anything, and that playing for the team was the only way I knew to fulfill my dream of playing college hockey.

The questions kept coming—the same questions ten to fifteen times with no new answers. I was getting more uncomfortable. I was tired and frightened and I just wanted to go to my room.

When he asked to examine me for a fourth time, he asked for me to take down my underwear as well as my sweat pants. I did. I was noticeably shaking and I flinched at his touch. The GM inspected my charley horse, groin, and stomach. Then it was over.

After what seemed like an eternity, he said that he could see I was tired and that I should probably go to bed and get some sleep.

Back in my room, I felt safe behind the closed door. I felt that I had somehow passed the test that he had given me and that I could never tell anyone about the questions he had asked me that night. I was sure that if I confided in my parents, they would make me come home. I knew that the best thing to do was to never talk about the incident to anyone, pretend that it never happened, and hope that it never occurred again. After all, my dream of a college scholarship might not be possible if I weren't playing Junior 'B' hockey.

Everything seemed to go better after that night. I ended up making the final cut and soon thereafter we began the season. I enrolled in grade 11 and started class on the second day of school. I became accustomed to the rules of the house and what my responsibilities were. Mind you, the atmosphere around the house and how people related to each other weren't what I was used to. My family was at ease with each other; they were stiff. My dinner table was a place to interact; in this house, it was simply a place to eat. But then, I hadn't expected other families to be like mine.

During the week, things seemed to follow that same schedule and I was able to fit into the routine without having conflicts with the GM. But the weekends were a different story. After work on Friday, he would start to drink. By the time the hockey game was over or his wife had gone to sleep, he would be well into his cups and he would offer me beer as well. This was his time for testing me. At least that's the way I thought about it in my mind.

He never asked those strange questions again—thank goodness—

but during most of these sessions he would try to back me into a corner. The best way I can describe it is that he was playing mind games with me for the purpose of controlling me. To what end I could only guess, but not knowing was as frightening as knowing.

Whether he talked about how poorly I was playing in recent games or about how unsociable I was with my teammates, he would start in on me quite harshly. I remember these conversations very well. He would stare at me and attack me on whatever front he had decided I was inadequate. These sessions would range from 30 minutes or an hour to long into the night. I knew that he was trying to test me, but I also knew that the only way to pass his little tests were to stare right back at him and stand up to his interrogation. He often threatened to tell my father about my poor performances—whether on the ice or in the class room—but he never did say anything to my father.

Another puzzling incident happened on my birthday. The GM gave me an expensive golf bag, a dozen golf balls, a Walkman, and my team coat. Christmas in September. No one else on the team had received his team coat as yet. It was awkward explaining his generosity to my parents.

As fall wore on and I became accustomed to the routine of living with a new family, the shock and fear of the first few weeks in this unusual environment wore off and I began to think I could handle the GM's bizarre behavior. That is, until he found out about my plan to go back to my high school in Michigan after the hockey season was over. He made a big deal about my commitment to the team and, besides, he was quite sure that it wasn't possible to leave the school in the middle of the term and expect to be able to re-enroll the next fall.

This upset me because I thought I could last only until the end of the season, not the whole school year. It was then that I decided that I would tell my parents at Christmastime about him and his mind control games. Hopefully, my record in Junior 'B' hockey would be enough to impress some college scouts.

That plan allowed me to rest easy at night until Halloween. For the holiday weekend, my parents had decided they would visit and bring my girlfriend, Heather Albertie, and my good friend, Keith TerHaar along with them.

Keith was invited to stay with me in my room at the house. After the game on Friday night, the GM kept both of us up until early morning with the same mind games. When he finally let us go to bed, Keith was shocked. Did this happen often? Was he always this way? This is more than weird, Keith said. Did my dad know about this? Keith said I had to tell him.

I knew what would happen if I told my dad, but I knew Keith was right. The mind games were beginning to wear me down. I think I was able to put up with it as long as I did because I knew that about 360 miles to the west, there was a home where I was loved and where I would be taken back in a heartbeat. I knew what the word "home" really meant.

When I finally did call my dad, my parents were ready to come like the cavalry to take me back. And before I knew it, I was "home." It was sad to leave the friends I had made in school and on the hockey team, but I knew I had to leave. I knew that this might cost me the chance at a college scholarship, but being subjected to his behavior wasn't worth it—even if I had to work my way through college mowing lawns.

Being home wasn't everything that I'd hoped it would be. It would not be easy answering the inevitable questions as to why I came home from Canada well before the end of hockey season. In addition, there wasn't any hockey going on in the area except house leagues that played only once a week. It also was difficult going back to high school because it was nearing the end of the semester. But then, there was the option of going back to Canada.

Once again it seemed as though I had a decision to make about how much I really wanted my dream of playing college hockey to come true. Did I want to stay home and take my chances with what hockey I could find for the next two seasons, or did I want to try going back to Canada to give Junior 'B' hockey one more try? Was I living this dream because it was what my father expected of me? Was I trying to achieve success in college hockey because my brother, Scott, had worked so hard and never seemed to be rewarded for his determination? I can remember remarking to my father that it seemed that every decision was bigger than the last one, even though the last decision was the biggest of my life. "Every decision leads into a new day full of new and bigger decisions," he replied.

"Gee. Thanks, Dad," I said.

After talking it over with my family, I decided that going to Canada had been the right thing to do regardless of what had happened earlier. So with fingers crossed and my bags repacked, my parents loaded me into the family van and we headed for St. Marys, Ontario. The experience that awaited me would turn out to be everything I had hoped Junior 'B' hockey in Canada would be.

Meeting the coach, Scott Graham, felt more like meeting a family friend than the coach of a hockey team. Mr. Graham showed us around the city of 5,000. After going to the rink (which seemed to have a seating capacity big enough to accommodate over half of St. Marys' population) and driving by the school that I would be attending, Mr. Graham introduced me to the family that I would be staying with. The Parkinsons already had one player staying with them, Scott Garrow. Like me, Scott was hoping to get a college scholarship.

Having Scott to show me around school was a bonus. He introduced me to the rest of the guys on the team and his group of friends. There was a handful of hockey players that came from out of town to play for the St. Marys Lincolns. These guys were my built-in friends from the first introductions.

St. Marys was a totally different situation from what I had experienced before. In St. Marys, half the town went to see the games. There were fifteen of us who went to school together so there was a ready-made group of friends at school. Everybody in the town knew who the players were and the Lincolns' games were big news. The result was a town of people who cared about the team and its players.

Playing in St. Marys gave me a chance to do what I had dreamed of from the day I went to Bowling Green and watched my brother suit-up for the Falcon hockey team—play college hockey. But it gave me much more than an excellent hockey experience. St. Marys gave me a chance to experience an environment of closely knit family-oriented people. The Lincolns were an organization that excelled on the ice, and also cared enough to make sure its players were diligent students. The Parkinsons, my friends, the school, and the members of the team quickly made St. Marys my home away from home.

Several things were different in the high school life of a Canadian teenager, versus the life I had known back in Michigan. The value students placed on education was considerably different in Canada. It was my impression from the schools in Michigan that college prep courses and advanced classes were only for the accelerated students. In Ontario, each student wishing to graduate with their grade thirteen diploma was required to complete six advanced courses. The level of these courses was such that they counted for credits at some American universities. It seemed that the majority of students participated in the advanced courses, and it was "not cool" if you decided not to graduate from grade thirteen, whether you were going on to a university or not.

The lack of emphasis the Canadian educational system placed on sports also surprised me. While sports were an important part of the high school, they did not dominate the atmosphere of the school as it does at so many American high schools. Although Canadians love their sports, there was more emphasis placed on classroom than athletics. Contests were played during the final period of the school day. Students who participated in sports were encouraged to schedule a study period during this last hour so each player wouldn't miss too much school. Students were only allowed to watch the games if their study periods coincided with the time of the game. Parental or community attendance was rare.

Because I had started the school year in Canada and had gone home in March to my high school in Michigan, I had to adapt from the classes in Canada to classes in Michigan halfway through the second semester. Although this seems impossible given the different syllabus, West Michigan Christian High School made special arrangements. The classes at W.M.C. were more difficult than the classes at St. Marys through the twelfth grade, but in order to get into a university in Canada you needed grade thirteen. Grade thirteen courses were as difficult as some of the classes I would take later in college. I won't make a widespread judgment that Canada's education system is better than in the United States, but it was interesting to notice a considerable difference between the two systems. My education certainly did not suffer by attending Canadian high school.

One other thing that took a while to get used to was the respect students showed to teachers. In Canada, the teachers are afforded the respect due to any professional occupation. It was standard procedure to address each teacher as "Ma'am" or "Sir." Although I had been taught by my parents to respect teachers, using such a formal address took a while to get used to. It also took a while to discard.

My most memorable education experience in St. Marys came from Mr. Ainslie—a physics teacher we affectionately called "The Mad Scientist." He quickly became my favorite teacher due to the circus-like atmosphere he created in his classroom. His antics included throwing a brick across the room. Mr. Ainslie had a passion for physics and an incredible knack for bringing the mysteries of gravity and angles of refraction into a resisting high school mind. In class he referred to me as "The Yank" and often his problems involved a Canadian rocket ship versus an American rocket ship. If I couldn't figure out the answer, my guess would always be with his Canadian ship.

Many students learned to love physics because Mr. Ainslie loved teaching. He developed a special way to make it fun. Mr. Ainslie found a unique way to transfer his love for his discipline and his job to the people around him. The result was a lesson and a person I'll never forget.

The experience in St. Marys was everything that my parents and I had hoped Canada would be. Not only did I get a chance to get a first-rate education and play for a winning Junior 'B' team, but there were quality people that had a very positive influence on my life. The Parkinsons took me in as one of their own children. My teammates and high school friends accepted me halfway through a season without questioning where I came from or why. The Goads, the family that I stayed with my second year, opened up their home to me as well. The friendships that I established in St. Marys will last a lifetime. One of my classmates, Tonya Stephens, and her family, became for me my family away from home. They gave me a taste of the family life from which I was 1,000 miles away.

Looking back, I find myself very fortunate to have been blessed with the people who welcomed me into their families and circle of friends. To each person I owe a great deal of gratitude. They all made what could have been a difficult time very easy.

Playing in the NHL haunts the dreams of every young aspiring Canadian hockey player. In Canada there are two routes to the NHL, Major Junior 'A' and Junior 'B'. These two leagues are similar in terms of age and quality of players, but there is one major difference. If you have the skills to potentially play in the NHL, Major Junior 'A' hockey is a better, faster route. However, if you play as much as one game of Major Junior 'A', you become ineligible to play U.S. college hockey. Many times the choice between playing Major Junior 'A' or playing Junior 'B' comes down to wanting to get a college degree.

Each spring, Major Junior 'A' holds a draft from among the sixteen-year-old players in North America. It is to minor league hockey players what the NHL draft is to eighteen-year-olds. During my Major Junior 'A' draft year the Lincolns had an exceptional year and several players were being scouted by Major Junior 'A' clubs. I had always thought that getting a college education was the key to one's future and would be a good thing with which to attack life after hockey. Dick Todd, the General Manager of the Peterbourgh Petes (now assistant coach with the New York Rangers), made Major Junior 'A' sound very tempting and that the NHL was a good possibility, but I stuck with my decision to work toward a college scholarship.

Many of my memories of St. Marys are of the people and friends who accepted me into their community, but I'd gone to St. Marys in hopes of gaining a college scholarship and play for an elite college program. The St. Marys Lincolns turned in two exceptional seasons and propelled several of its players into college hockey and the Major Junior 'A' ranks. For me, the Lincolns provided the chance to play on a team that obtained enough points to win the league title. In that first year with the Lincolns, the team was made up of mostly veteran players (seventeen-, eighteen-, and nineteen-year-olds) with just a few younger players. Being one of the youngest players, not only did I get a chance to play for a winning team, but I had the opportunity to play with older, more talented players. It was a true learning experience.

In my second year in St. Marys the makeup of the team changed to a younger team of rookies and second year players. It was an opportunity for me and the young players from the year before to increase our contribution and provide leadership roles on the team. I remember getting called into the office of the General Manager of the team and being told, "The organization is counting on you and young Scotty Garrow to provide enough goals for us to repeat as league champions." As I left his office, I wondered if what I was beginning to feel for the first time was pressure.

As the season began, the pressure to lead the team and score gave way to the pressure I felt from the college scouts in their overcoats that lined the top row of the arena at each game. The year before they had been there to talk to the group of Grade 12 players that had hopes of playing in college. But this year was the year I hoped they would be talking to me. Sometimes you would hear a rumor about a certain school being in the stands. Sometimes you would only hope that the right school was watching the right game.

During my first year, recruiting letters came occasionally, but they were usually pretty standard:" . . . we saw you play, our program is looking for solid recruits, keep up the good work, etc., etc." Sometimes I received the same form letter *twice*, just to let me know they *really* cared.

My second year, the recruiting process really cranked up, and it started right from the first exhibition game. Sometimes coaches wanted to talk after the game. Sometimes they called me at home and the letters started coming from everywhere. I narrowed my choices to Bowling Green State University (BG), the University of Michigan, and Western Michigan University.

After talking with each school's coaches, judging where I might fit in each program, and getting an overall feel for each university, I decided that I would make an official visit to B.G. and Western Michigan and choose between the two. I was very impressed with the show Western Michigan put on when I visited and I was leaning toward going there. Plus, I felt that Coach Wilkinson was a good man and a great competitor.

But I grew up a fan of Bowling Green hockey and always dreamed of wearing #21 for the brown and orange, my brother Scott's number when he played there. After several phone conversations with my parents, it seemed like Western Michigan was the smartest choice for my career both on the ice and in the classroom. But once again sleep was the ultimate test. I just couldn't sleep with the decision to go to Western, and ultimately it came down to simply feeling more comfortable with the people at Bowling Green and my desire to continue the legacy my brother had started.

My parents had always stressed the importance of a good education and getting good grades in school, but this was even more apparent during the recruiting process. Every questionnaire asked about high school grades and college entrance tests. Every college coach asked about my grades as well, and stressed how important it is to keep up with your studies once you got to college. Sometimes college coaches didn't even ask about hockey or comment on the game I'd just played in. At times, I actually felt that certain coaches weren't that interested in me as a player because they didn't seem too interested in my hockey.

Looking back, I realize that hockey was just one of the things that college coaches were interested in when it came to evaluating recruits. During recruitment, the college coaches had three questions that were standard when they called Junior 'B' general managers. What are the young man's grades, what kind of kid is he, and what kind of player is he? The order was just that: grades, character, and ability. The character issues came before hockey. Why? A big part of being a college hockey player, at least in the minds of coaches, is being able to handle the college scene and keeping focused on maintaining good grades. Certainly, being able to compete on the ice is a factor. But you can't compete if your grades keep you ineligible, and you won't be allowed to compete if you're in and out of trouble and a poor reflection on the program. Being successful *on* the ice often depends on being successful *off* the ice. Character matters.

The backyard rink where it all began for Dan.

Even though he was just a toddler Dan was always involved in the family games on the backyard rink. Later Dan would become serious competition for his big brothers.

Before he was two years old Dan possessed a great love of sports.

At age three, Dan was copying, the older boys' golf swing.

Dan's freshman year in golf didn't start well.

Practicing his short game in the backyard.

This Muskegon Pee Wee team won the Big Rapids Tournament.
Dan is in the bottom row, second from the right.

Dan won the High School State Golf Championship in dramatic fashion, sinking a
birdie putt on the last hole. This was his freshman year. His brother Jon, who was
also in the tournament, celebrates Dan's victory in the background.

After deciding that he wanted to play college hockey Dan left Grand Haven for St. Marys, in Ontario, Canada. He played for the Junior "B" Lincolns his junior and senior years of high school. He hoped a successful career in Junior "B" hockey would lead to a college scholarship—and it did.

The Lincolns typically drew crowds of 1,000–2,000 fans at home games. After his final game, a Lincolns fan told Jay Bylsma "that kid is going to play in the NHL one day."

Although he did not play back home, his Canadian classmates believed every American kid could shoot hoops. They encouraged Dan to play for St. Marys.

Dan was the Lincolns' leading scorer in his senior year. Here he posed with his trophy while displaying his wallet-photo of Kirk Gibson.

During high school baseball games Dan hung his poster of Detroit Tiger star Kirk Gibson on the dugout wall to give his team "the Gibby Blessing."

A thrilling moment for Dan, at bat in Detroit Tiger Stadium during the Michigan High School Coaches East-West All Star Game.

Dan followed in his brother's footsteps and attended Bowling Green State University. With Scott's #21 on his jersey, Dan drives around the net against Lake Superior State. #23 Sandy Moger is also a current Los Angeles King.

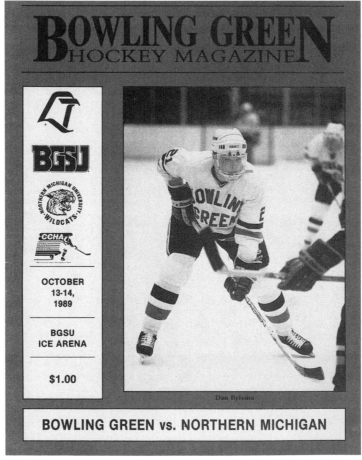

The cover of Bowling Green hockey's weekly program featuring Dan in his sophomore season.

Dan's first minor league team was the Monarchs in Greensboro, North Carolina. The other East Coast Hockey League franchise was named after the team in the movie Slapshot, *the Chiefs, from Johnstown, Pennsylvania.*

With a new arena under construction the Greensboro Monarchs started their 1992 season with the longest road trip in professional hockey—16,500 miles—in this bus. Dan is pictured top left.

Dan, a Moncton Hawk at the time, seems pretty confident here, while friend and college roommate Ken Klee looks a bit concerned. Klee and his Portland Pirate teammates got the best of Moncton in the Calder Cup final.

*Rochester and Albany were
brief stops along the road to
the NHL.*

Playing in Phoenix resulted from Dan's first NHL contract, and was close enough to finally believe his dream of making it to "The Show" would come true.

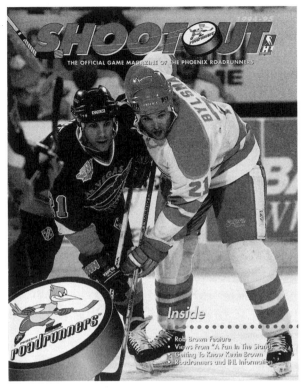

Blocking shots is Dan's stock-in-trade. He is considered one of the Kings' best penalty killers.

A defensive specialist applying skills learned in college and honed in the minors, Dan battles along the boards.

"While playing on the penalty kill, Bylsma is always outnumbered, but never outmanned." Bill Plaschke—LA Times

Dan's college teammate, Rob Blake, is also a current member of the Kings. Blake took a different route to the NHL though. Shortly after he left Bowling Green State University after his junior year he was taking regular shifts for Los Angeles.

Four years and seven minor league teams after graduation,
Dan finally makes it to The National Hockey League.

3

COLLEGE

JAY

College baseball didn't last long for Dan. Just as the exhibition games were to start in the fall, the hockey team began its dry land training. The hockey season then lasted until after the baseball team left for their spring trip to Florida. Dan decided that he had enough to handle with hockey and academics so, after the fall try-outs his freshman year, he abandoned college baseball.

There were seven freshman forwards coming into the hockey program at B.G. that fall. Seven forwards to fill five spots, so there would be some sitting out. But Dan played in 39 of 46 games. He played some on the second and third lines but mostly did duty on the fourth line. He had four goals and seven assists and made one highlight film—he scored two goals in the space of thirty seconds in the last game of the regular season.

My assessment of the season was that his play was spotty. His skills were there, but he needed some maturity. What we did not know until Dan got to college was that many of the hockey players had played Juniors one or two years out of grade thirteen. So Dan not only was the youngest player at B.G. but one of the youngest players in the league.

When the 1988 NHL draft came around that summer, we paid scant attention to it until Scott called to say that Dan had been drafted in the sixth round—106th overall by the Winnipeg Jets. Scott added, "It looks like he might be in the NHL someday." Nancy and I just looked at each other when we heard.

Danny, Danny. What will become of you?

Dan went back to Bowling Green the fall of his sophomore year with a renewed determination to improve. During training camp, he worked his way into the second line as the left wing playing with a junior, Marc Potvin and a highly touted freshman, Bret Harkins. Dan began the season on fire, which included a hat trick against Western Michigan (two of the goals were short-handed). After six games he led the team in goals with six, ahead of Nelson Emerson, B.G.'s candidate for the Hobey Baker award—the Heisman Trophy of college hockey. He was making the highlight films. B.G. had two formidable lines in Emerson's line and the Bylsma, Harkins, Potvin line.

When practice started the following week in preparation for the November 22/23 series against the University of Michigan, Dan called to say he had been put on the third line. Coach York had praised his play and said they needed to improve the third line, the checking line. With Dan's size and defensive ability, he was the guy to do the job.

Although I didn't let Dan know, I was not only disappointed, I was furious. The second line had been playing well and Dan had been playing better and better each week. I was afraid what this would do to his confidence. Secretly, I also was afraid of what this would do to his numbers, to how good he would be *perceived* to be. Numbers tell a story. He had six goals and five assists in the first six games. From then on, playing on the third line, he scored seven goals and had twelve assists in 33 games. From one goal a game to one goal in every five.

During his sophomore year, because of his hard work and hustle, he was assigned to the penalty killing unit. While killing penalties (playing when one or more of your teammates is in the penalty box) is not as glamorous as playing on the power play (when one of your opponents is in the penalty box and you have a better chance to score), Dan saw it as an opportunity to be noticed. He began to block shots. Over the course of three years, he came to be one of the best penalty killers in the C.C.H.A. He scored two short-handed goals in one game against Western Michigan University and in another game against W.M.U. he scored a goal while his team was playing two men short.

At the time, I lamented the fact that he didn't get the more glamorous roles of playing on the first line or playing on the power play—roles which I thought his hard work and talent earned for him. On reflection, the "opportunity" to play on the penalty killing unit, and the development of skills to kill penalties and block shots was his ticket to the NHL. In contrast, the players in Dan's class who were the big scorers, largely because they played on the power play, Peter Holmes (26 goals, 34 assists) and Martin Jiranek (25 goals, 28 assists), never saw the NHL. Holmes and Jiranek received the flowers; with these stats they were selected to the All-CCHA Second Team.

Based on the way All-Conference teams are selected, Holmes and Jiranek were logical selections and Dan was not. The point I wish to make is that not being on B.G.'s power play when he was as prolific a scorer in even strength situations as either Holmes or Jiranek could have soured Dan on his coaching staff, on the game, on the media, and on the CCHA selection committees. Rather, he used the opportunities that *were* presented to him and worked hard to excel in those areas. He had learned, "I can't do anything about the things over which I have no control and I can't worry about those things. I can affect the things over which I have control; those are the things I need to work on."

What could have been perceived as a roadblock to success (being assigned to the penalty killing unit instead of the power play), he used as a ramp to the NHL.

It's interesting to me that of the eighteen players selected to the

All-CCHA First, Second, and Honorable Mention during Dan's senior year, only four have played the equivalent of a full season in the NHL; Keith Jones (325 games), Sandy Moger (132), David Oliver (155), and Brian Smolinski (281). Seven of the eighteen honorees never played in the NHL. Bill Wilkinson is right, " . . . it's only flowers."

Dan did get some flowers. He was a B.G.S.U. Scholar Athlete in each of his four years (at least a 3.0 grade point average and a letter winner in a varsity sport). He was a selection to the All-CCHA Academic team in his sophomore and senior years and Honorable Mention as a Junior. He won the Jack Gregory Award for the highest grade point average on the team in his sophomore season (Scott was honored with the same award as a senior). And in Dan's senior year, he was selected to receive the Howard Brown Award, the coaches' choice of the player most exemplifying hard work, leadership, and citizenship. He also was elected to the Bowling Green Chapter of Omicron Delta Kappa, an honorary fraternity to which members are elected on the basis of outstanding character, leadership, and scholarship.

There were many proud parental moments experienced from Bangor, Maine to Fairbanks, Alaska over his four year career. Nearly every weekend, we followed the fortunes of Dan and the Bowling Green Falcons. I think the only times we missed were for Laurie's choir concerts or to see her portray a very sassy Molly, the smallest moppet, in her high school's production of "Annie."

It also was a proud moment to watch Dan receive his college diploma, just as Scott, Greg, and Jon had received theirs before him. He had earned his Bachelor's Degree in Business Administration with a major in accounting in four years with better than a 3.0 grade point average.

So your son wants to play in the NHL, some other major league or wants to rise to the top of his profession? Or you are a young athlete with dreams? The most important thing you can do to help your children or to help yourself to get to "the show" is to get good grades in school. Why good grades? When Dan was playing Junior 'B' and was being recruited by college coaches, the first question out of their mouths after the introductions was "So, what's Dan's grade point average?" or "What are Dan's A.C.T. scores?" Unless your last name is Gretzky, if you couldn't answer with high enough G.P.A.s or scores, the inquirer would be polite, talk about the weather this time of year, and leave you to direct his attention on some other lad whose G.P.A.s or scores met his college's minimums for admission. *That's* why good grades are of utmost importance. And remember, there aren't many Gretzkys. Good grades can open doors, they can reveal character that will often separate you from others of equal ability.

Another reason why education is so important is that there is life after hockey, and that for all but a very few, life after hockey comes sooner rather than later. Only a percentage of the kids that play Bantams (13–14 year olds) play Midgets (15-16). A very small percentage of the kids that play Midgets will play Juniors (17 - 20). Of the players who make it to Juniors, only a very small percentage of those will play college hockey. From all of the kids Dan played with in St. Marys, only Scott Garrow also played college hockey. That's *two* out of about thirty-five players.

Of all the players in the CCHA who graduated in 1992 with Dan, only ten ever played in the NHL. Of those ten, only three played the equivalent of one full season (at least 82 games) as of the 1996/97 season (five years out of college). There were other players from this class who jumped to the NHL before graduation, but it is indisputable that only an infinitesimal percentage of boys who play in local rinks realize their dream to make it to "the show." And from that infinitesimal number, only a few are fortunate to make a career of it.

Failure is the rule for which success is the exception. Therefore, the most important thing your son can have if he fails to make it to "the show" is a good education.

DAN

From the time I called up Coach York (B.G.'s hockey coach) and told him that I planned to join the Falcons, I began imagining what it would be like to wear the brown and orange and take the world by storm. Part of the recruiting process is building you up into what they hope you will become when you choose their school. It's also part of a seventeen-year-old's ego to believe that you'll dominate in college just like you did for your Junior 'B' team.

So, at the end of August every year, a handful of freshmen full of vim and vigor converge on campus (where they are indistinguishable from Adam) and join players who've already established themselves in the college ranks. It's an interesting couple of months for immature young adults trying to find their way in a world full of new experiences.

Before the hockey season begins there's the matter of settling into your schoolwork and deciding how you're going to react to the new-found freedom that the first year away from any authority figure brings. It's a dilemma trying to decide where your schoolwork ends and your free time begins. Maybe that's why the coaches are so concerned with grades and personality before they decide to offer a scholarship.

Although the team can't officially be on the ice before the end of September, off-ice training begins immediately upon arrival at school. The team starts to mold itself into a working unit from the first day. This isn't always an easy process, considering the fact that every player coming into the program was one of the best, if not the best, player on his previous team. The older players feel it's their responsibility to break down snotty-nosed freshman egos just like the upper classmen before them broke down theirs.

As a freshman, you have so much to learn on and off the ice. Upper classmen believe it is their responsibility to provide you with a crash course. Some of it—like learning how hard you need to work off the ice on strength and conditioning, and learning new skills on the ice that make you a better all-around player—is helpful. Some of it—like learning that you have to fill "your veteran's" water glass after every practice—isn't so helpful. Making sure your meal tickets were available for "your veteran" when he stops by was another "rule" I didn't like. In addition, a party is held in "honor" of the incoming freshmen which eliminates any individuality a player might be hanging onto and makes him realize the team does not exist to showcase his talents alone. I'll spare you the details; it was ugly but I survived.

After months of preparation, the season finally began. At least, it began for the team. I could occasionally be found in the stands doing statistics. By Christmas break I had played in only half of the games and I was struggling to find a place on a team with stars like Rob Blake (now a teammate with the Kings) and Nelson Emerson (now with the Carolina Hurricanes). I was beginning to wonder if I had made a wrong decision about the college I had chosen or about playing college hockey.

During one of the many phone calls I made home, my father steadied me. "Hang in there and work hard," he said. "Be prepared and keep a good attitude. Your chance will come." Slowly, his advice came true. After a solid performance during a Christmas tournament, I was rewarded with a regular spot in the lineup for the rest of the year.

Although we had a team that was filled with All-Star players, we never seemed to find that necessary chemistry that propels a squad toward championships. We did get a bid for the NCAA tournament, but Boston College spanked us in the first round. It ended a season of disappointment not only for the team, but especially for me. My plans of coming to Bowling Green and quickly becoming a factor in college hockey turned into working hard just to stay in the lineup.

Although the hockey season had been dismal for me personally, two things happened that changed me as a player. Early in the year, I was struggling with the fact that I was not contributing on the offensive end of the rink. Coach York was quick to spot my frustration and pull me into his office for a meeting. "Did I ever tell you the story of the cat and the dog?" he asked. "Offense is like a cat, and defense and hard work is like a dog. You can call the cat, but it only comes around when it feels like it and sometimes it ignores you. You can never count on it.

"The dog, on the other hand," Coach York said, "obeys its master much better. When you call a dog it comes. Don't worry about your offense, sometimes it'll come. Sometimes like the cat, it will elude you. Make sure your hard work and defensive play is like the dog, always there when you call on it." His little story helped me to realize that I could contribute at both ends of the rink. Sometimes you couldn't control the bounces and breaks in the offensive end of the rink, but how hard you work and your defensive play was always under your control.

Another meeting I had with Coach York that year was much harder to stomach. After the season, the coaches met with each player to evaluate the season and talk about what could be done to improve over the summer months. My meeting after that freshman season was one I would have liked to forget, but couldn't.

The coaches took turns describing the reasons they brought me to B.G., and then proceeded to tell me how I hadn't measured up; how I lacked the skills necessary to be an effective player at the college level; how they weren't sure where I fit in the plans for next season and worse still, they weren't sure I possessed the necessary drive to improve on my weaknesses.

I needed to be a better skater, I needed to be stronger, and I needed to be more aggressive on the offensive end of the rink. I took it all in and didn't say a word. The reason I didn't open my mouth to speak was I'm sure if I had, I would have broken down and cried. I saved that until I got back to my dorm room. It was then that I wrote down exactly how I felt. All the anger I felt for the three coaches who had just painted a dismal picture of my sorry freshman year and who had only given me a glimmer of hope for my remaining three years. With tears of humiliation and anger rolling down my cheeks, I expressed my frustration at not having performed to my capabilities. I had been told I was inadequate and I had come to the stark realization that they were right. I hadn't lived up to my own expectations and I hadn't proved that I could compete at the college level on a regular basis.

In my anger, humiliation and frustration, I made a promise to myself. I promised that I would never let anyone be able to say those things to me again. I would never let someone say that I hadn't worked hard enough. I would never let anyone say that I hadn't lived up to my potential. I would never let anyone say that I didn't have the determination or the drive to do what had to be done. I was hurt, I was mad, and I didn't ever want to feel that way again.

I vowed to turn that anger into the necessary drive to do what it took that summer to be ready for a much improved sophomore season. I made a plan right then for the whole summer, outlining exactly what I was going to do and how I was going to do it in order to come prepared for the next season. From strength training four times a week to plyometrics and running, I was going to make sure that I would be in the best physical shape of my life. I also dedicated two weeks of the summer to going to a camp for college and pro players that specialized in improving skating quickness.

I was going to be ready, physically and mentally, for the next season.

During the school year I had turned 18. It meant that the summer after my freshman year I would become eligible for the NHL draft. After my disappointing season, being drafted wasn't even on my list of concerns. In fact, draft day came and went without my even knowing it. The next morning, my oldest brother, Scott, called and informed me that I had been the ninth pick in the sixth round by the Winnipeg Jets, 106th overall. A dismal first year had me wondering if I had a role on the team . . . now an NHL team drafts me.

When the next season rolled around, I was determined to have my second year be a reflection of my true abilities. After a strong training camp both on and off the ice, I started the season on one of the top two lines, and six games into the season I was leading the team in scoring with six goals and five assists. I was on the C.C.H.A. highlight films, and I felt I was taking the world by storm. And then disaster struck.

At the beginning of week four, Coach York brought me into his office and told me I was going to start playing on the third line. He wanted to make the third line more defensive-minded. As it turned out, it was a great move for my professional career. But at that moment I couldn't understand it.

I had sat in his office six months earlier and listened to him tell me that he wasn't sure I could play college hockey, how my skating needed to improve, and that I had been a disappointment. I had worked my butt off trying to prove him wrong and I did. Now this was how he was going to repay me. This wasn't a matter of being passed over for flowers, this was a demotion—a demotion I didn't deserve.

"Control what you can control." Those words were whispered in my ear again and again by parents who were sure that this was just another opportunity disguised as a setback. But how many opportunities disguised as setbacks did I need? Not being chosen for the Select camps, the incident with my first GM, a poor freshman year, and now my removal from the scoring lines.

At that point, who would have thought that seven years later Dan Bylsma would be in the NHL because of his play as a defensive forward?

I know I didn't say, "Thanks" back then nor did I want to. But "Thanks," Coach York.

Another event that changed my life forever happened during my freshman year in Geography 125 class. I sat in the seat directly behind my future wife. I may not have learned much about geography that semester, but I did meet Mary Elisabeth Friel, a young lady who six years later would say "Yes" to my marriage proposal.

She was one of Bowling Green's most talented gymnasts and she was equally talented at flirting. Because B.G. hockey players socialized with the gymnastics team, I got to see her outside of geography class as well. From the beginning of our sophomore year, we spent a lot of time together, but only as friends. She became a regular at the hockey games (Section A, Row 2, Seat 2) and I began to learn about the balance beam, floor exercise and back flips with round-offs.

When I met Mary Beth, I didn't see her as someone that I would want to marry. I even told her several times that we would never go out on a date. I thought of her as a friend, a friend that I enjoyed spending time with. Before I knew it, though, I realized that I was *finding* time to spend with her and that she was someone with whom I could share everything that was happening in my life. And that, I found, is a fairly good recipe for a good marriage partner.

After my freshman year, not only was I disappointed with my play but my playing time as well. I hadn't been given any time on the power play or the penalty kill. Don't get me wrong, my play didn't deserve it. But finding a way to get more ice time was one of my goals in my sophomore and junior years. After talking it over with my dad and brother, Scott, I decided that trying to work my way onto the penalty killing unit was the way to get more ice time.

During the power play practice that the team went through on a weekly basis, the extra players were asked to kill the penalties. When I got the opportunity I tried to do whatever it took to get noticed. "Whatever it took" ended up meaning blocking shots.

In my junior year, I had started to develop a knack for getting down in front of shots that were taken on a power play. It slowly turned into an increase in ice time. Little did I know that trying to find some way to get more ice time would turn into a specialty, a specialty without which

I would have never gotten close to the NHL. Remember, defense is like the dog ... always there.

I chose Bowling Green University because its hockey program was known for a strong winning tradition and a knack for getting their players into the pro ranks. It disappoints me to say that the program didn't win any championships with me in the brown and orange, but I did see many of my teammates reach the pro ranks and twelve made it all the way to the NHL.

Looking back at my college career, I know that the course my coaches chose worked out for me in the long run. At the time, I didn't want to be put on a defensive line and I would have chosen to play a more glamorous role on the power play—not slug it out on the penalty kill. But after my meeting during my freshman year, I learned (they forced me to learn) that hard work and defensive play are abilities that must be a part of your everyday attitude. You can't control a lot of the things that happen around and to you. So it's imperative you control the things you can control. Attitude, work ethic, and defense top the list.

One of the great things about college is the number of opportunities and resources that are available to student athletes. It's also one of the bad things. College life is filled with many decisions about personal conduct both in and out of the classroom. The balance between one's social life and academic life usually determines success, or lack thereof, in the class. It can also determine one's success, or lack thereof, in the arena.

For an athlete, other complicating factors are thrown into the mix. Student athletes have to contend with a restricted time schedule depending upon the demands of their particular sport. In addition, there are the pressures of having to perform in front of the whole school and sometimes the country on national television. You might also get to read about your successes and failures in the newspaper. Handling the adulation that accompanies being a sports star can be pleasantly distracting.

This is not to say that the student athlete should be cut any slack. These complicating factors are part of the bargain in accepting scholarship money in exchange for your services in the arena. Therefore, coming to college with a moral compass, good study habits, a healthy sense of responsibility, and a lack of self-importance is essential. Character matters and it matters a great deal.

Just as important as performing well in hockey is excelling in the classroom. My brothers before me had graduated from major universities with enviable grade point averages. My parents and family were concerned about my hockey career, but they always were eager to ask about how well I was doing in school. After all, I still had to open my report card in front of my father. My siblings weren't that interested in my academic achievements but they were happy to point out that they had gotten an A in Calculus when I had only gotten a B+.

In Scott's senior year, he received the Jack Gregory Award for the hockey player with the highest grade point average and that was an award that I desperately wanted to achieve before I left B.G. I was very happy on the day in my sophomore year I was able to call Scott and let him know that my name had joined his on the award.

Perhaps even more satisfying, however, was the fact that the same coaches who had berated me after my freshman year for not having enough drive to improve my skills, awarded me the Howard Brown Coaches Award after my senior season. This award goes each year to the player who best embodies the characteristics of hard work, dedication, and improvement.

Although the Bowling Green hockey program had a long and rich winning tradition, during my senior year our team managed only nine wins and missed the playoffs for the first time in ten seasons.

For four years, I walked to our locker room past the photographs of the ex-Bowling Green players who had made it to the NHL. But only in my sleep had I dared to think that I had a chance to get my photo on that wall. Now I had agents calling me, telling me that Winnipeg would be interested in a contract. It was possible, they said, that the Jets might be prepared to sign a deal at the end of my season. A small part of me was hoping the end of a dismal season would somehow come sooner than expected.

Star players had agents who negotiated big deal contracts. Now I had a handful knocking at my door, wanting to sign me as one of their players. Signing with an agent means they have rights to negotiate a contract on your behalf in exchange for a small percentage of your deal. After asking around and doing some homework on agents and what agents could and couldn't do for their clients, I interviewed several and decided, along with my parents, that we had no idea which agents might be good or even how to spot a bad agent. On my dad's advice I picked the one that I had a good feeling about, the one that I felt had the most integrity. My choice was Lewis Gross.

Lewis contacted Winnipeg to see about the possibility of my joining the Jets even before the school year had ended. The Jets seemed to have some interest in the idea so I began waiting for the call to pack up and leave for my new life in pro hockey. Right about that time, the NHL players decided to strike. When the season resumed, it seemed that the Jets had a lot of other things to worry about. But promises during the summer of getting a deal done kept me thinking that becoming a pro in the fall was what was in store for Dan Bylsma. At least that was the reason I gave my dad for not interviewing for any after-college accounting jobs during the spring semester.

Even though B.G. didn't make it to the playoffs, I was invited to attend the awards banquet that is held each year at the finals of the C.C.H.A. playoffs. I had been selected to the C.C.H.A. All-Academic team along with five other players in the league. The selection honored each player for outstanding achievements not only on the ice, but for diligence in the classroom as well. It was an award that I took great pride in winning my sophomore and senior years.

At the end of the spring semester of my senior year, I walked into the B.G. football stadium to graduate from Bowling Green State University. With my parents and sister sitting in the stands, I received a B. S. in accounting. That day was important to me because my parents had instilled the value of education in their children, and it was reinforced by my brothers who earned their degrees in respectable fashion. A few years after I got my degree from B.G., my sister Laurie got hers from Michigan State University.

I can't close the chapter on my college career without acknowledging the support that I received from my family. If it weren't for them, I wouldn't have had a college career. In addition, they drove thousands and thousands of miles to watch me play, show their support, and be there with a roll of Lifesavers (actually, it was a post-game pizza) whenever they thought I needed it. When time and distance allowed my brothers to get away, they came to my games as well. Laurie was in high school when I was in college and quite often came along to be a supportive little sister. She dyed a bra burnt orange and wore it to my games to indicate her "support." On an occasion when I was invited back to my high school to give a chapel talk (to her embarrassment *and* secret delight), I acknowledged her gesture by pulling the orange bra out of a bag. If my brothers ever wore burnt orange underwear, I was not aware of it.

4

MINOR LEAGUES

JAY

There are some players who are *wunderkinds* and know when they are playing Juniors or are in their first few years of college that they will be superstars in the NHL. For most, however, the road to the NHL is not a straight line. There are two examples from among Dan's teammates at Bowling Green State University: Rob Blake and Nelson Emerson. Blake was a defenseman during Dan's freshman and sophomore years. A fourth round NHL draft choice, he was big and fast, could handle the puck well, and had a strong shot. The morning after the last game of his junior year, Blake had a plane ticket to Los Angeles and within a few days, he was taking a regular shift with the Kings and has never looked back.

Nelson Emerson was a classmate of Blake's and a third round draft choice. He was Bowling Green's most prolific scorer ever and one of the leading CCHA scorers of all time. Emerson had to spend a year in the minors before making it in the NHL.

For Dan, the road to the NHL was a lot longer, far more circuitous and filled with several potential career-ending disappointments. It all began the day after his last college game. He engaged an agent, Lewis Gross, who contacted the Winnipeg Jets. There was some discussion about Dan leaving school and joining Winnipeg. It was all very exciting until the NHL Players' Association went on strike. With the NHL shut down, the Jets' discussions with Dan's agent were terminated. We were very disappointed for him.

A while later, Winnipeg contacted Gross to see if Dan would be willing to cross the picket line if the NHL decided to finish the season with "scab" players. Gross's advice to Dan was that hockey was a very physical game. If Dan had any thoughts about eventually playing in the NHL, he could count on the striking players having long memories and short tempers when it came to replacement players. Dan decided to decline the offer to cross the picket line. When the owners decided not to attempt to field teams during the strike, Dan's decision became moot.

The strike was settled in early summer of 1992, so Dan was filled with expectations about attending his first NHL training camp with Winnipeg. It was another disappointment when a letter arrived that explained that, due to additional costs associated with the strike and the settlement, the Jets were limiting the size of their training camp. Dan was instructed to report to the Moncton Hawks, the Jets' American League affiliate in Moncton, New Brunswick, in the fall.

Throughout the summer, Dan trained like he had never trained before. Weights (two days on the upper body, two days on the lower body), and a three mile run nearly every day. All the while, he was walking up to twelve miles a day mowing lawns for Jim Dykstra.

Dan also became one of the chaperones for a venture of a group of young people from our church. The group spent a week in Appalachia building homes for Habitat for Humanity. A longtime friend, Tom Hammond, also was a chaperone on that trip.

When the group returned, Hammond took me aside. "That is some son you have there," he said. "He took charge of the group from the first morning, young people and adults alike. When we woke up in the morning, he gave us the 'saying of the day.' Things like: 'If you want to make footprints in the sands of time, wear work boots.' He would also quiz us each day on the saying. He was so up-beat and positive; the kids just loved him. So did the adults. He made the trip for me. It was a neat experience just to be around him."

The saying of the day. It was always some quote he had read or heard that gave him some inspiration or insight. Some of the other sayings of the day were, "No one is promised tomorrow, so do what you can today" (Walter Payton), and "Every job is the self portrait of the person who did it." They were little bits of wisdom he used to keep his focus, to keep the important things in perspective. Wisdom he could pass along like snacks for the soul.

Several times during the summer he received calls from Jeff Brubaker, the coach of the Greensboro (North Carolina) Monarchs of the East Coast Hockey League (ECHL). Brubaker said that if the opportunity with the Jets didn't work out, Dan was welcome to play for the Monarchs. It was a good thing to know.

After Dan left for Moncton, we followed his reports on training camp with great interest. He liked Robby Laird, Moncton's coach. Yes, these players were, on average, better than college players but he thought he could play at this level. When the exhibition games began, we could tell his confidence was growing. He led the Hawks in scoring in the exhibition season, and on the morning following the last game, Laird summoned Dan to his office and said the five favorite words in a rookie's vocabulary, "Find a place to live."

He was very excited when he called to tell us the news. It was a Monday, and the season was to start on Thursday. Thursday morning he called again. "Dad," he said, "I'm coming home."

I couldn't believe it. "You're coming home? What happened?"

"The Russian Hockey Federation just released their players to sign NHL contracts," he said. "The Jets signed six Russians. There is no room for Dan Bylsma."

"Dano, I'm so sorry. What will you do?"

"Call Jeff Brubaker in Greensboro and try out there, I guess."

In spite of the huge disappointment, Dan collected himself and called Brubaker. The Monarchs welcomed him and he began the season in Greensboro. Certainly, it was not the opportunity he wanted but it *was* an opportunity. And instead of reeling from the fickle finger of fate that was flipped at him, he went to work to make the most of it.

Because the Greensboro Coliseum was being renovated, the Monarchs' first nineteen games were on the road. Dan was part of setting a professional hockey record for the longest road trip—over 16,500 miles. All of it was on a bus.

Just like he had in Canada, Dan moved in with a local family. Bill and Nancy ("Neal") Bolton boarded him and made him a part of their family. The salary rate for the season was $250 per week, with expenses paid, and the tenure of the contract was day to day. It was enough, *if* you thought it was only a stepping stone to better things.

As a parent, I have never been at ease about where Dan was until I actually saw his surroundings for myself. Until I saw the arena where he played, visited the locker room, saw the house where he lived and the bedroom he slept in, he was disconnected from me. This "dis-ease" festered inside me and became more acute each time I spoke to him until I was able to travel to see his world for myself. After I saw it, I was able to visualize what he was talking about when he described the events of his life. Then it was a part of my life, too. So, we traveled to Greensboro. Yes, to see Dan. But more importantly, so I could see his world.

He did well in this Greensboro world of his. He scored twenty-five goals and assisted on thirty-five others. He killed penalties and played on the power play, and his hard work won him a nomination for the ECHL Rookie of the Year Award. He was named the team's Most Valuable Player, and he got called up to play two games for the Rochester Americans in the American Hockey League (AHL) where he had an assist. When Scott heard about the MVP award he said, "Mark my words, he's going to be in the NHL someday."

At the end of the season, Dan came home to his now familiar summer regimen of mowing lawns during the day and working out at night. That summer he again chaperoned a group of young people from church, this time to the projects of Chicago, assisting people in the refurbishing of their apartments.

During the summer, the Greensboro Monarchs became affiliated with the new expansion team in the NHL, the Mighty Ducks of Anaheim (California), a team owned by the Disney Corporation. As one of the top players for the Monarchs, Dan was invited to attend the Ducks' inaugural training camp. Attending an NHL training camp and the possibility of moving up from the East Coast League was an exciting opportunity.

Dan reported back from Anaheim nearly every night. Yes, it was a great experience. Yes, he thought he could play at this level. But in the end, the coach called him in and told him that he had a great camp but not good enough to dislodge any of the players under contract. They thanked him for coming and wished him luck in his career. It was yet another disappointment.

In our conversations, it was very difficult to give him the support he needed. My words were hollow, my advice stuck to the roof my mouth like so much peanut butter. I wasn't there, I didn't know the situation he faced firsthand. My son had a goal, a dream, and he had been so close he had tasted it. Yet, he was so far from his dream I wondered if it might be an illusion for him, an unholy grail. Difficult for me; more difficult, I was sure, for him.

Dan decided to go back to Greensboro and give it his best shot for one more year. He was back to his MVP form, scoring fourteen goals with sixteen assists in his first, and what would be his last, twenty-five games in the East Coast League. Again he was on the power play, he killed penalties, he blocked shots, he worked hard, he hoped someone was watching.

On December 8, 1993, Dan got called up for a three game stint with the Albany River Rats of the American Hockey League. Albany is the farm team of the New Jersey Devils. Although he only accounted for one assist in the three games, he thought he had played well. The River Rats indicated they were considering recalling him for the following weekend, but they also said that they had called him up on the condition he would return to the Monarchs for an important game the following Wednesday. So they were obliged to send him back for the time being.

On Wednesday, December 15, 1993, Robby Laird, the coach of the Moncton Hawks called. Dan was to be in Moncton on Thursday for an indefinite stay. Santa Claus had come early! Dan had clawed his way back to the point where he had started his professional career, the farm team of the Winnipeg Jets.

Jeff Brubaker later reminisced about what he saw in Dan. "It was immediately apparent when Dan came to us that he was a quality person. We were surprised that someone of this caliber had filtered down to the ECHL. The fact that he was a million miles from the NHL did not seem to lead him into the rut that most players in this league get into—consumed by the feeling that they had too far to go to make it. Dan seemed to operate on the theory that if he did everything possible to become the best player he could be, someone would notice and he would get a break. He was right.

"When he finally made it to Moncton" Brubaker said, "we got reports back that Dan was figuring out what it took to get to the *next* level and how to make the most of his unique talents in order to make himself valuable to any team he played on.

"Dan's unique ability was that he was a fearless shot-blocker. He had less fear of going down in front of a 100 mile-per-hour slap shot than some goal tenders. This shot-blocking ability was the first thing that caused people to take him seriously as an NHL prospect."

So your son wants to play in the NHL? Brubaker did not say Dan stood out because of his talent. Brubaker noticed the quality of his character, his never-say-die attitude, and his ability to figure out what it took to advance to the next level. Your parenting must be in life skills, the application may be in hockey.

Dan flew home for Christmas and I met him at the airport. He had played a few games for Moncton but hadn't scored yet. We talked about how he was doing and what his expectations were. I said to him, "This is your father talking. Would an honest appraisal of your chances for a career in this sport indicate it's time to think about getting a real job?"

Dan replied, "I *know* I can play at this level. I think I can play at the *next* level."

"The NHL?"

"The NHL."

When Dan joined Moncton, they were in last (sixth) place in the Atlantic Division of the AHL and had the worst record in the AHL. Craig Fisher, a goal scorer who had played for Miami of Ohio in the CCHA, was acquired at the same time. The addition of Fisher's scoring and Dan's defensive play and penalty killing helped the Hawks to third place in the division by the end of the season. In the playoffs, the Hawks won their division and went on to the Calder Cup finals where they lost to the Portland Pirates in six games.

The trip to the Calder Cup finals was a bittersweet ride. Sweet because he was in pursuit of a championship, although a championship appeared improbable when he and Fisher joined the team. Sweet because he was a significant part of the team's success. Bitter because there were rumors that Winnipeg was going to terminate the relationship with Moncton as its farm club. If that were to happen, it was speculated that the Moncton Hawks would cease operations and Dan would be out of a job.

The rumors and speculation proved to be true. Moncton, which had appeared to be a source of hope, became another disappointment. Dan came home after the Calder Cup finals and began mowing lawns for Jim Dykstra.

I couldn't help but wonder how much disappointment he could take and still be his ebullient self, still retain the self-confidence so necessary for an athlete or anyone in any line of work to perform at his best. How many times would the wounds scab over?

His play at Moncton and particularly in the playoffs had attracted some notice and two NHL teams or their affiliates were in discussion with Dan's agent. One was the Detroit Red Wings. The coach of their farm team, Newell Brown, had been engaged as a scout for Moncton for the playoffs. The other team was the Washington Capitals, the parent club of the Portland Pirates. I learned after the playoffs that the Pirates' scouting report on Dan was that he was very highly respected by Portland, who felt he had to be neutralized if Portland was to win the Cup.

During the discussions with Detroit and Washington, Rob Laird called to ask if Dan had signed with anyone yet. Rob indicated that he was being considered for the head coaching job with the Phoenix Roadrunners of the International Hockey League, the Los Angeles Kings' farm club. If he got the job, he wanted Dan to come, too. He thought he could get him a contract with the Kings.

Laird got the Phoenix job and Dan got a three-year, two-way contract with the Kings (one salary level if Dan played with the Kings, a lower amount if he played for Phoenix). Was his dream coming true? It was an NHL contract. It was for three years. It meant going to training camp with Wayne Gretzky, his childhood idol. At the least, it meant a three-year stint in the International Hockey League. At the most, it meant becoming a Los Angeles King. The emotional roller coaster ride began again, this time on a bigger coaster. Scott was quick to remind me of his prediction. "I told you he'd be in the NHL someday."

Much later, I had the opportunity to ask Rob Laird why, of all the players in Moncton, did he choose to take Dan along to Phoenix. His reply was, "When you evaluate players, you look for three basic things; outstanding offensive skills, outstanding defensive skills, and the ability to win. A good player will have at least two of these characteristics. In Dan's case, he's an outstanding defensive player and he knows what it takes to win. Knowing what it takes to win is intangible, but a coach recognizes it when he sees it. It's working harder in practice than you have to. It's riding the (training) bike longer than required. It's being able to call up reserves in a critical situation. It's being willing to sacrifice yourself for the team; in Dan's case, being willing to put his body in front of slap shots. It's putting the team before yourself. It's being a leader. Dan excels at these intangible things. That's why I wanted him to move with me to Phoenix. That's why I believed Dan could make it to the NHL.

"Another thing about Dan," Laird said, "was that he had a win/win attitude. Professional sports is a very competitive atmosphere. For the most part, guys have a win/lose attitude. By that I mean, for me to win—that is, for my career to advance—*you* have to lose. Therefore, most guys don't help to improve other players' games. It's every man for himself. Dan's attitude was to help anyone he could to make the team better. He went out of his way to make rookies or newcomers feel welcome and help them get settled. He seemed to have the attitude that if we win as a team, we all win—all of our chances of advancing to the next level improve. And I think he's right.

"Also, Dan came to play every game and worked hard every shift. One guy like that on a team forces other players to step up their game by his example."

So your son wants to play in the NHL? So you want your child to excel in business? Hear what Laird said. First, Dan had a specialty—he excelled at being a defensive player. That came from taking a road block and making it a ramp when he was assigned to the checking line and penalty killing unit instead of the more glamorous first line and power play unit in college. Second, Dan knew what it took to win. Laird described that as having a good work ethic and being unselfish. I believe that came from the backyard, Dan's interaction with his brothers and an understanding of what it takes and the desire to improve. Having what it takes to win, being willing to help other players, and working hard, are character traits and attitudes about life absorbed by the child from his environment that carry over to sports or whatever field the child chooses for a career. The preparation is for life, the application may be the NHL.

DAN

The summer following my graduation from college, I returned to mowing lawns for Jim Dykstra for the seventh year. It was not Phi Beta Kappa work but I didn't have any better job opportunities, and I was waiting for that contract I knew would be coming. What I didn't know was how involved the negotiating and signing process was. After the NHL playoffs come to an end, teams assess their players and start preparing for the draft that happens at the beginning of July. Although Lewis Gross called Winnipeg and inquired about signing me to a contract, the Jets insisted that they would be ready to talk only after they sorted things out and the draft ended. I did what I could to fill the time and to train for getting the chance to play pro hockey.

I lifted weights four times a week and tried to get in a cardiovascular workout at least three times a week. It was the same regimen that I started after my freshman year in college. I was preparing, but the draft had come and gone and the Jets didn't seem eager to sign a deal. Lewis didn't seem to be panicking, but I was getting a little nervous about what the fall would bring. By the middle of August, all I had was an invitation to come to training camp and I was beginning to get the feeling that maybe the contract wasn't coming. About the time I was sure Winnipeg had forgotten me, their front office called. I was informed that owners all around the league were trying to cut costs and the Jets were going to cut costs by limiting the number of players that they would be inviting to camp. So I was told to report directly to their farm team in Moncton, New Brunswick.

I had understood that playing in the minors was a possibility when I turned pro, so going to the Jets' minor league affiliate in the AHL wasn't a major disappointment. At the beginning of September I packed my bags and ventured off to New Brunswick and the Moncton Hawks. What I didn't realize were the hazards of going to camp without a contract, even a minor league camp.

Moncton started training camp on September 12 without many of the players that would be coming down from Winnipeg when the Jets started to make cuts. I felt comfortable from the start and was able to establish myself in practices and intrasquad games. I would call home to inform my parents that I had a good practice and had even scored on the good goalie. As players arrived from Winnipeg, the roster started to fill up and fewer and fewer spots were available. When preseason games started, I felt I was playing well. In a game against the Cape Breton Oilers, I had a goal and an assist in a 4–2 Moncton win and was named the First Star of the game. I couldn't help but feel that I was taking the right steps toward making the team. By the close of training camp, I had managed to increase my statistics to two goals and three assists and the coach had indicated that I should start looking for an apartment.

Just in case they tried to spring a deal on me, my agent was preparing me to negotiate a contract by myself. Lewis thought Moncton might try to corner me in the coach's office and get me to sign a deal that was less than fair. Well, I got called into the office . . . but it wasn't to negotiate a deal. The coach, Rob Laird, informed me that the Jets were going to send down one more player and that meant they didn't have room for me on the roster.

I was shocked and couldn't believe what I was hearing. During preseason, I led the team in scoring and played better than some of the guys under contract with the Jets. First they tell me to look for a place to stay, then they tell me I'm going home. It was my first lesson in how pro hockey works. First, contracts rarely get done until the last possible moment when the player feels most vulnerable. Second, going to camp without a contract is fighting an uphill battle; a hill that turns into Mount Everest, a battle like Bull Run. I sat in the stands for the Hawks' first game in a bewildered state. I couldn't help thinking that I knew I could play out there and I couldn't help wonder where I would end up playing hockey.

The plane ride home provided me with too much time to think. Had I tried hard enough? Was it maybe time to put my accounting degree to work? Was not making the AHL a sign that I wasn't as good as I believed myself to be? Maybe, I thought, it was best if I just hung up the skates and concentrated on getting a real job. My dream of playing in the NHL had hit its first major roadblock and it was time to test my mettle.

I knew I was capable of playing *at least* at the AHL level and I knew I could add something to a team. I decided that I would give hockey, wherever I wound up, everything I had. I didn't want to end my career when I knew in my heart that I could play at that level. If I was good enough to play at the AHL level, and if some of those players had played at the NHL level, well then, you never know. It was time to set new goals; time to battle back.

By the time my plane arrived back home, Lewis had already secured a spot for me at the camp of the Greensboro Monarchs, a team in the East Coast Hockey League (ECHL). I was still reeling from my experience in Moncton when Lewis gave me the news that Jeff Brubaker, Greensboro's coach, expected me as soon as possible. I spent a couple of days hunting grouse with my dad. The resplendent autumnal colors, the sight of a Gordon Setter bird dog working the coverts, the wild flushes of the grouse, and the time alone in the outdoors with my dad was good medicine. It was good to go back to my roots, the source of much of my strength and now a source of healing. It was a time to lick my wounds and put the disappointment that professional hockey had handed me into proper perspective. I regrouped, repacked my bags, and I headed for Tobacco Road.

I arrived at training camp just as it was coming to a close, but I still had to establish myself as an integral part of this ECHL team (the ECHL is two steps down from the NHL—the equivalent of baseball's Double A league). I thought I could be an impact player and hoped to get called up to the AHL or the IHL as soon as possible (both the AHL and the IHL are one league down from the NHL—the same as baseball's Triple A league). What I wasn't ready for was what I saw when I entered the locker room that first day.

It was a sight I had only seen in my brother's men's league locker room. The first three players I saw were not only sporting more paunch than muscle, they were smoking. As I found a seat in the back of the room, I couldn't help but wonder if I was getting into a remake of the movie *Slapshot.*

One of the most unforgettable experiences of my pro career happened at the beginning of that first year. Luckily, I didn't know any better and I was just trying to take everything in stride. The Greensboro Monarchs' home arena was undergoing renovations and we were scheduled to start the season with a *19-game* road trip. We weren't slated to play a home game until early in December. Although we had a custom-designed bus to ease the pain of travel, nothing could have made that road trip to hell and back bearable.

Over the course of two months, we traveled 16,589 miles and saw a total of 22 movies. We traveled from Birmingham, Alabama, to Toledo, Ohio; from Knoxville, Tennessee, to Roanoke, Virginia, and from Erie, Pennsylvania to Raleigh, North Carolina. Some of our trips lasted for 12 hours.

The bus had two television sets with VCRs, a captain's chair for the coach, and couch seats over half its length that faced each other. Beyond the couches there was a table with bench seats and a small kitchen with sink, stove, and refrigerator. The "facilities," including a shower, were at the rear of the bus. To my knowledge, no one used the shower.

During long stretches, each player would assume his customary position on the bus. These spots were determined by the pecking order on the team and it was based on games and years in the league, who were the big shots or leaders—sometimes just on who got to the good seats first. Some guys were always jockeying for position at the card table, which is where I was most of the time (a.k.a. the kitchen table), but most were just glad to get a good spot on one of the couches. The couches folded down to make one large mattress.

What a sight it was to see twenty people trying to grab some shuteye lying head-to-feet and feet-to-head. By the end of a twelve-hour bus ride, you either became real close to some of your teammates or you got real sick of them. These days, when I settle into my leather seat on the chartered plane of the Los Angeles Kings, I can really appreciate the luxury that's available to players in the NHL.

About the same time I arrived in Greensboro, another player in a similar situation joined the Monarchs. His name was Davis Payne. Both of us had finished college with hopes of signing an NHL contract and working our way to "the show." Together we decided that the only way out of this league was if we worked hard and improved on the things that we didn't excel at. We felt that we were capable of playing at a higher level and believed that given a chance, we'd prove it. Whether it was because of the circumstances or our similar situations, Davis became my best friend in hockey.

From the beginning, I knew that fighting was going to be a part of the game that I really hadn't experienced in college. I had fought a few times in Jr. B, but now there would be no face masks protecting what little good looks I had. Two days into our season, Coach Brubaker grabbed Davis Payne and me and asked if we had ever been taught the ins and outs of fighting. Having come from college, neither of us were pugilistic wonders. "Bru," on the other hand, was a man whose face belied any notion that he made his living in professional hockey as a finesse player. He looked like we should be taking lessons from his *opponents*.

"Fighting fair was no way to fight at all" was Bru's #1 rule. "You'll win

80% of your fights if you get the first punch in," he said, "so don't wait around for something to happen. Throw the first punch with your glove on, with it off, or start it with an elbow. But whatever you do, don't start it fair."

He showed us tactics on where to grab and how to punch. Bru's Rule #2 was, "At the end of the fight, no matter how bad the guy rang your bell or how bad you rang his, always pick yourself up and skate to the penalty box as fast as you can. Let the other guy know that he didn't hurt you and you're ready to go again."

This wasn't a one-lesson tutorial. There was continuing education. Occasionally, he would come around after practice and pick fake fights with Davis and me. During one of these "tutorials," one of Davis' rights jabs got away from him and landed full force upside Brubaker's well-battered face. After a moment of awkward silence (as Davis watched his life flash in front of his eyes), Bru shook his head as if to clear some cobwebs and smiled. "I forgot how good that felt," he said. Right then I knew why Coach Brubaker had made it as a tough guy in the NHL and that I never would.

When the season started for the Monarchs, I found myself in the stands. I was told that some players still needed to be cut before room was made for me on the roster. Whatever the real reason was, the bottom line was I didn't dress for that first game. Even after I played my first four games, I found myself sitting on the bench much of the time. I was beginning to get fed up with what this game had to offer. I had gone from hopes of getting a contract and going straight to Winnipeg to just getting a letter inviting me to training camp. Soon that changed into going to a minor league affiliate's training camp, now down to playing sparingly at the ECHL level. I was frustrated and I was beginning to think that even accounting might be better than what pro hockey had to offer Dan Bylsma.

I told Coach Brubaker that I thought I could contribute more to the team than I had in the first four games. I understood that everybody couldn't be used in every situation, but I had performed well in training camp and felt confident that I could play a major role for a team at this level. Coach Brubaker explained that he was using players that had proved themselves the previous year and that he felt comfortable with certain players in certain roles. He said that I would have to prove my-self to him just like they had. When our little meeting was over, I wasn't sure it had done me any good. The next game, though, I played more and in different situations and I scored a game-tying goal late in the third period. From that point on, I started to be a regular contributor for the Monarchs.

At the beginning of the year, you signed a contract for whatever amount (in my case it was $250 a week). This contract could be termi-nated at any time and the team's obligation was only up to the day of termination. The team also was responsible for providing you with a place to live, whether an apartment or a billet. In my case I lived with the Boltons, a wonderful family that had a lovely home. I had the run of the basement and was invited to become a part of their family.

The East Coast League was primarily made up of two types of play-ers. One group just wanted to play hockey for a few more years and get a chance to travel. It wasn't a bad idea because the cities usually treated the players very well. The perks alone were enough to keep some play-ers around for a few extra years. The other group of players (surpris-ingly, a minority) were interested in working their way into a higher league. The ECHL was just starting to become a developmental league for the "A" and the "I," but very few players were signing contracts and leaving "The Coast" forever. Davis Payne and I desperately wanted to make it to the next level and even dared to think that we were capable of playing in the NHL. We made a deal that we would push each other to work harder after practice and in the gym. It was the only way we would improve and stay focused. You never knew when our games were being watched by an NHL scout. You just hoped they were.

The season slogged along and, at times, I thought I was playing well enough to get the call up. At other times, frustration took over and I wondered if I was just hanging on to a boyhood fantasy. Adjusting to the length of a professional season added to the consternation. In college, we competed in 35 to 40 games over a six-month period. A pro sched-ule might total more than ninety games, including exhibitions and play-offs, over six or seven months.

On February 20, the call that I always hoped would come—that I was beginning to think might never come—came. Coach Brubaker informed me that the Rochester Americans of the AHL needed a player for a few games and that I was going to be it. I was filled with anticipation and the hope that a few games would turn into something more. I packed a few things and flew to Rochester to join the team before the bus ride up to Hamilton, Ontario, Canada. I wasn't certain that my family could be there to see my first AHL game, but it wasn't a surprise when I saw them in the stands. What *was* a surprise was the speed of the game. The players were bigger and faster than the players in the ECHL and I found myself just trying to keep up with the pace. I can still remember hearing the national anthem and how nervous I was.

My stint ended after two games, but two things were very clear to me after I went back to Greensboro. I was capable of playing at that level, and I had a lot work to do in order to be more prepared for the next call up —especially in terms of my skating quickness.

As the year came to a close, I focused most of my extra work on drills to increase foot speed. Unfortunately, the Monarchs lost a one game playdown to get into the playoffs and summer came sooner than expected. Once again, though, summer came with the hope that I would sign a contract with either an NHL, AHL, or IHL team.

As usual, I was working for Dykstra Landscaping and going to the gym trying to improve on my leg and upper body strength and my foot speed. Lewis Gross was busy on his end trying to contact teams that may have been interested in signing a forward for the upcoming year. Things didn't get moving until after the draft, but there was some good news. The Portland Pirates, the Washington Capitals' AHL farm team, was interested in signing me to a contract. After the draft was sorted out and Washington knew how many players they would be sending down, they would probably need one or two more forwards.

I felt confident that this would be the break I needed. I knew I could play at that level and that all I needed was for a team to give me a chance. Lewis and the Pirates had started to talk about when the deal might be done and a salary range. Although nothing had been signed, I was getting excited about the prospect of stepping up to the next level. My luck had to be changing because the good news was rolling in. The

Anaheim Mighty Ducks entered the NHL and announced that Greensboro would be their affiliation in the ECHL. Because Anaheim was interested in evaluating the talent in their farm system, another Greensboro player and I were invited to the Mighty Ducks' inaugural training camp. I hoped that this might give me an opportunity to impress an NHL team.

Going to an NHL training camp would be a chance to see how I stacked up against the best players in the world. Although I didn't have a contract, I was sure they'd be looking for players for their minor league team. I wanted someone to notice me, someone who would be willing to give me the chance I needed.

Training camp was difficult. I had never practiced at such a high level. The speed was dizzying and the passes were hard, tape-to-tape passes. I had to bust my butt just to keep up, but I didn't feel as if I was over my head. I thought I was making a good showing and even had the coach pass pucks to me and put me through some extra work after practice.

At the end of the first week, we had an intrasquad game that was open to the public. We dressed in the new Ducks uniforms and played in front of a full Anaheim arena. What a high it was! The clock was ticking, there were referees, we were in real NHL uniforms and the stands were filled with screaming fans. At that moment, I knew I wanted to make it to the real thing. More importantly, I felt that I was as good as some of the players out there. If these guys played in the NHL, then I certainly could, too. The only thing they had that I didn't ... was an NHL contract.

Two days later my fantasy came to an end when I was called into the General Manager's office for the "Thanks-for-coming-you-played-well-sorry-all-our-contracts-are-filled" meeting. I was disappointed, sure. But then, it was my first NHL camp. What did I expect? Besides, I had Portland to fall back on. Right? Waiting for Portland's call turned out to take more than a day or two. In fact, I'm still waiting for Portland to call. Lewis informed me that the Capitals had sent down more players than expected so there was no room in Portland. It also was too late to hope for a contract from another team. I had been available all summer and no one seemed to be that interested. Since camp for Greensboro wouldn't open until October 13, I had a lot of time to ruminate on all the possibilities that hadn't happened.

Doubts as to whether I would ever get the chance to move up

clouded my mind. I began to wonder how long I could keep holding on to the dream. Did playing hockey for $250 a week make sense when I had a degree in accounting and could make real money elsewhere? On the other hand, I believed that I wasn't through improving. I had just been to an NHL camp and I was sure I was as good as some of the players that had played in "the show." Besides, I was having a great time playing hockey. Who knew what could happen if I finally got a chance? I was determined to give hockey another try so I decided to play in the ECHL for one or two more years before it would be time to take the accounting degree off the mantle.

We came out of camp that year in Greensboro with a respectable team. We talked of becoming one of the best teams in the league. Winning might draw attention to our team and to my play. As an additional measure, Coach Brubaker brought in a sports psychologist in hopes of installing a winning attitude.

The psychologist's message was pretty basic. If you wanted something to come to pass, you needed to make it your #1 priority. If running a four minute mile was the most important thing in your life, your mind would find a way to get your body to do it. What it took was commitment. It almost seemed too simple, but as a team we decided to give it a try. Before the season began, we committed to winning seventeen of our first twenty games. We looked at the schedule and thought that seventeen wins was a difficult but obtainable goal. We won sixteen.

As an individual, I liked what the sports psychologist had to say. I was looking for something extra to bring to my game and maybe it was adding more intensity and more commitment. As a result, I made some personal goals that I thought would improve my skills and visibility. I would become a better skater, improve my shot, work on driving to the net and work on becoming a more physical player. My commitment was to make it to the next level, the AHL or the IHL, and then to the NHL. On the advice of the sports psychologist, I started a journal. It was a way of charting my improvement and progress along the road to my ultimate goal, making the NHL.

The best way to explain what happened over the next few months is through this journal.

- November 7, 1993. *It's a new time for me. I started writing to collect my thoughts and simply to keep me more focused on the game, my goals, and my dream. I will look back on this entry as the turning point of my professional career, for tomorrow I'll be taking one step closer to the NHL. I am a creative goal scorer. I am a power forward with the ability to drive the net at all times. I am one of the best defensive forwards in the league. Work hard in practice on my shot, driving the net, and do extra skating drills. Promise: Tomorrow you will be one step closer to the NHL.*

- November 20, 1993. *I'm ready to get back on the scoring track tomorrow. I'm starting to gain that confidence that I can be a big factor in the outcome of the game. Tomorrow I'll be one day closer to the NHL.*

- November 26. *I had a disappointing practice. I couldn't stay focused on the drills we were doing. Have to concentrate on working on the individual aspects of my game as well as the team aspects. Tomorrow, I will concentrate on the things that I can improve on: skating, shooting and driving the net. Davis and I went to the gym today and got in a workout (chest, back and arms).*

- December 3. *I played better, but still need to make some better shooting decisions. Take your time when you get the puck. Patience is the key to making good plays. We won 5–4 and took over first place. Yeah!*

- December 5. *We beat Hampton Roads 5–2. I finally scored. Yes! Good Night.*

- December 7. *Practice was tough today. Gave some extra attention to skating and quick feet drills. In the evening Davis and I attended the USA versus USSR exhibition game. I think I could've held my own out there. Went out to Buffalo's after the game.*

- December 8. *Tonight we beat South Carolina 6–5. I had two assists and played fairly well. Didn't have breakfast before the pregame skate and had mac-n-cheese for a pregame meal. Napped for about 1 hour and 45 minutes. I talked to my sister Laurie this evening. She seems to be doing well in school. Today I got one day closer to the NHL.*

- December 14. *I've missed several days because I got called up to Albany. I played three games. I thought I played real well. I played the* body, went to the net hard, shot the puck when I got the chance, and got the puck out every time it came around the boards. I thought I played well, I hope they got the same impression. I almost felt comfortable and I am once again assured that I can play at that level and make a difference. Today practice went pretty good. I know I have to pick up my play, not only in the games but in practice as well. Maybe I can get in better shape.

- December 16. I'm on my way to Moncton. After a series of phone calls and running around, I left Greensboro at 3 p.m. On to Boston and then to Halifax where I am staying in a hotel. Hopefully, this is the break I've been waiting and working for. Keep going and work hard and the chips will fall my way!

- December 18. Yesterday I flew from Halifax to Sydney and joined the team for a pregame skate. I had one practice to get used to the new equipment, including new sticks. The game against Cape Breton went pretty well. We won 2–1. I played a respectable amount, but not a lot. I penalty-killed and we didn't let them score. I got in a fight, a draw I guess. I hear something is happening in Winnipeg. Hopefully, they will open up a spot for me.

My confidence is high. I feel like I am close to putting some points on the board in this league. I know I can; it's just a matter of time. I'm one step closer to the NHL.

- December 19. Had toast and coffee for breakfast and rode to practice with Craig Fisher. I was on a line with Fish and Deuce. Hopefully, it means something good. I know I can score and play well in this league, especially with these guys as my line. After practice I worked out with Kenny Gernander.

- December 20. Had toast and coffee for breakfast. Practice was pretty good and I am still on one of the top three lines.

- December 21. An interesting thought: Today, tomorrow, this week, this "chance" is not the beginning of my career, nor is it the beginning of my dream. It's another day, another game, another chance, another step along the road that I chose at the age of fifteen. The road that I've continually decided to follow at various points along the way, the road that has shaped the last nine years of my life. I've made it to this point because of the decisions I've made, the time and hard work I've put in, and the sacrifices (joys) incurred. So this chance is not the turning point, it's another decision to work hard, to excel, to attempt to stand above the rest. The turning point was the first decision; this is just another step. All previous steps led to this one and this point shall lead to . . . well, that is up to me, for me to decide. How hard will I work? How far will I allow myself to journey? Today, I am one step closer to the NHL.

- December 22. It's actually the 23rd today. I went out after the game last night, so I couldn't write. Toast and coffee started the day before the morning skate. After a nice and easy skate, I had lunch at the Pasta House with a couple of guys from the team. Read a little bit and couldn't fall asleep. The game went well. The team won, 3–0. My legs didn't feel so good, but I played a solid defensive game. I probably blocked eight shots including several in the last couple minutes to help save the shutout. At the offensive end, I'm really close to getting good scoring chances. It'll come, I just need to be patient. I think I'm beginning to earn a spot on the team. A couple more games like that one and I'll be on my way! See ya in the NHL.

- December 31. I've been home for Christmas and back again. The team is 5–0 since I've arrived from Greensboro. Today, I went to an optional skate and then back to the hotel. After going to the mall for some groceries, I stayed in the hotel all day. I went out to Fat Tuesdays for prime rib and then back to the room for the rest of the night. Happy New Year!

- January 1, 1994. We won again. The Hawks are 6–0 since I've been here. I hope it hasn't gone unnoticed. In tonight's game, I played good defense, checked their top line and held them to no goals, but I was –1. The penalty kill was 100% (0 for 8). I blocked five shots and had seven hits. I would like to score, but I'm still playing real well. One step closer to the "the show."

- January 3. Today was an interesting day. After practice and a bike ride, Coach Laird told me to find a place to live. Last time he told me that, within hours I was going home. Today, Lewis told me Winnipeg wants to sign me—finally. I'll believe it when I sign on the dotted line. After calling home and telling the family, I went to dinner and a movie with Claude (an old teammate from Greensboro who now lives in Moncton). For real: I'm one step closer to the NHL.

- January 4. *I just don't feel confident about anything. Except for the fact that I know I can play at this level. I know that I can play in Moncton and be a key player for this team. I deserve to play because I've worked hard enough. I'm talented enough. Keep believing in yourself. I'll score this week, guaranteed.*

- January 5. *Practice was relatively easy today. Slowly I'm gaining confidence offensively. It's something I need to believe in. I have the ability. It's coming out and it will show itself with hard work, both mentally and physically. It will happen. After practice I worked hard on shooting and stickhandling. It's important that I work hard and believe. Hopefully, tomorrow will be a big day. Fact: I'm one step closer to the NHL.*

- January 6. *Waited for a telephone call that never came (news that I have been offered a contract). Oh well, patience.*

- January 7. *Still waiting for the call, it probably won't come today. I hope I don't have to wait until Monday. Ate lunch at Len's again and dinner at Fat Tuesday again. Tonight, I can't forget to think about my confidence. I know I can score at this level; just go to the net and work hard.*

- January 11. *After lunch (you guessed it, at Len's) I watched some TV and read in the afternoon. I'm waiting for a call from Lewis. I hope it comes. I'm getting awfully nervous about my destination. I believe in my abilities as a hockey player. I know I can positively affect any team in the AHL. I will sign a contract because I deserve it.*

- January 13. *We played last night in Saint John and lost 5–4 in overtime. The game-winning goal came with eleven seconds left. The game-tying goal was an awful goal. I didn't get a point and was even on the night. Well, I finally signed the contract I've been waiting for: $35,000 Canadian. I'm waiting for next year's deal to come. I knew it. I always believed it. I always worked for that goal and now it has come true. Now my goals are reset for a new level, to the top, to the NHL. I know I can get there, it will happen. It is at the tip of my tongue, and it's so close I can almost taste it. And I will!*

Joining the Moncton Hawks turned out to be a defining moment in my career. Becoming part of a team that was in last place in the AHL in early December, working together—somehow righting the ship—and turning the team into one that had one of the best records from December on was something each one of us felt good about. With the addition of Craig Fisher, Wayne Doucet, and me, the team found a winning formula and started to believe that we could win every game. Although our poor record early in the season prevented us from getting home ice in the playoffs, a great run over the last three months put us in great position. No one wanted to play the Hawks in the first round, and we felt confident we could do some damage in the playoffs despite our third place seed (third out of four in our division).

I hadn't been on a winning team in a long time and in sports it is well known that careers are often made by teams performing well in playoffs. Players from playoff champions would often sign lucrative contracts and had great a chance of moving up to the NHL. It was rumored that fifteen players from the previous year's Calder Cup championship team(the AHL equivalent of the Stanley Cup) signed NHL deals after they won.

Playing in the playoffs gave me my first experience with the rigors of a seven-game series and it also gave our team an opportunity to label each one of us as winners. What I didn't have a clue about was the added intensity and pressure that come with the playoffs. Going from preseason to the regular season provides a similar jump and going from the ECHL to the AHL also provided a similar jump. But in order to get a good idea of what playoff hockey can inspire in teams and players, you need to multiply the jump in the level of intensity exponentially.

The pressure of every game and sometimes every play can be suffocating. The amount of pain that players are willing to play with, and the sacrifices that individuals make just to play the next game, is astonishing. Having gone through several seven-game series, sometimes (especially in the later rounds) it becomes a battle of attrition and perseverance more than a game of skill against skill. It becomes more mental than physical and the will to win becomes a performance-enhancing drug.

After the end of the season we began to prepare for our first round opponent, the Saint John Flames. Practices became shorter but the tempo was higher. The drills were designed to assimilate the Flames' game plan. The coaches started to have meetings with individuals, lines, and the special teams. The media hype started to apply added pressure. The papers started mapping out what we needed to accomplish in order to win the series and advance. The players just wanted the puck to be dropped to begin Game One. We traveled to Saint John for the first two games and hoped we could win one of the two.

It hardly worked out that way and before we knew it we were looking at an 0–2 advantage for the Flames heading back to Moncton. A few things quickly became apparent about playoff hockey. Every time anyone touched the puck, it was a chance for the opponent to put a lick on the puck carrier. Every time anyone came in front of the net—with the puck or not—it was an opportunity for the opponent to put a lick on that player. The theory being that over a seven-game series, you aggravate, frustrate, and eventually wear that player down. It doesn't take long for bad feelings to develop between players and teams and, in this case, the Hawks despised . . . no the feelings went deeper than that . . . *hated* the Flames. Truth be known, I have never gotten over those feelings against many of those players.

We knew if we won our home games we'd only have to win one in their building so that's what we set out to do as we headed back home for Games 3 and 4. That's just what we did, as we evened out the series with two close wins at home. Etched in my memory is the feeling we had in the locker room after those wins. Grown men jumping around hugging and screaming as if we all just won the lottery. What I also remember is the physical appearance of the team. Faces started to hollow out and beards started to fill in. We started to resemble a platoon of soldiers more than a hockey team. The injuries some players played with were well beyond what they would have—could have—tolerated in the regular season. You were expected to play with pain and it would have taken an amputation to take some guys out of the lineup.

Before Game 7 in Saint John, I remember at least three players going into the trainer's room before the game to get injections. What those players were willing to sacrifice for the team, and for a chance at winning, left a lasting impression on me.

From the beginning of the series we kept talking about just having to win one road game and all of our home games to win the series. We didn't panic when we got down two games to zip, we didn't panic when they won Game 5 to be one game from eliminating us, and we didn't panic when we had to go back to Saint John for Game 7. We knew we'd have to win one game on the road and what better way to do it than in Game 7 in their barn.

As the series dragged on, the pressure mounted with each game. By Game 7, the pressure was so great that every player knew that the next play or next decision could determine the outcome of the series—a fraction-of-a-second mistake sends you off for summer vacation . . . or handle it properly and you're on to the next round of the playoffs. The game became more a battle of stamina and endurance than a hockey game. It also provided the individual highlight of my playoff career. It was halfway through the second period of Game 7 on a four-on-four situation. Andy Brickley got me the puck just over the red line. Not having much else to do with it, I drove the defenseman wide on my backhand. Going to the net, I fired a low shot and the puck found its way over the goal line. Shortly thereafter, we got another goal and the fire slowly went out for the Flames. Seven games had taken their toll on both teams, but the Flames seemed unable to put up a last stand and we won the right to play the St. John's Maple Leafs (not to be confused with the Flames from Saint John). Not only was St. John's the team with the best record in the league, but they had easily beaten Cape Breton 4–0 in their first round playoff series.

We had battled it out with the Flames and now we had to deal with a fully rested St. John's Maple Leafs. To make matters worse we had to go St. John's for Games 1 and 2 and if need be, Game 6 and 7. Even though the Maple Leafs had a tough building to play in, we made it our goal again to get one of the first two games. Although we let the first game slip away, we played a great Game 2. At the end of regulation in Game 2, each team had only managed one goal. Halfway through the first 20-minute sudden death overtime, the puck slid by a Leaf defender allowing for a two-on-one break with me and Ken Gernander, my roommate. I was carrying the puck as we crossed center ice and I knew full well that I was going to pass. As the defenseman slid over to take away the pass, I flipped the puck over to Kenny and he shot it over the goalie's left shoulder. I can only remember being too tired to join the mob that engulfed Kenny G.

What a position we were in, heading back to Moncton 1–1 and having three home games ahead of us. Playing in the friendly confines of the Moncton Coliseum, we dreamed of three wins in a row to close out the series. So much for wishful thinking. We got out-played in Game 3 and lost 6–2. The Hawks battled back with back-to-back wins, including a 2–1 double overtime marathon, to return the series to St. John's. The series was becoming another drawn-out battle. Less and less it mattered how much skill each team brought to the table, and more and more it was becoming a battle of will and endurance. Heading back to St. John's up 3–2, we began to think we had a chance to win the series. Even though the Leafs out-played us and were leading by two goals halfway through the game, Game 6 turned out to be a one-line effort by Moncton. A spectacular effort by the line of Craig Fisher, Andy Brickley, and Ross Wilson overcame the two-goal deficit to gain a 4–2 series win. What a feeling! Totally exhausted in a roomful of grown, sweaty men— bruised, battered, and victorious.

We had played well in the first series against the Flames, but now we were gaining momentum. It seemed that each player was finding a new gear. Andy Brickley, Craig Fisher, and Arto Blomsted had each elevated their games, somehow coming up with big plays just when we needed a lift. We felt we were the team to beat even though we didn't have home ice and even though (on paper) we didn't have players to match up with their skill players. We knew we would find a way. Whether it was Ken Gernander in overtime or Ross Wilson in double overtime, we felt something snowballing.

Before advancing to the finals, we had to defeat the Cornwall Aces in a best of three miniseries. The series was over about halfway through the first game when the Hawks took a two-goal lead over the Aces and the wind went out of their sails. We made quick work of the Aces, finishing them off 5–1 in Game 2.

Into this pressure cooker that was the playoffs came a breath of spring in the late Canadian winter of 1994. It was a calming touch in my competitive world of smelly hockey gloves and sweaty bodies, and a reminder of what was important in my life. Mary Beth came to stay for the rest of the playoffs. Her flirting finally began to pay off; we were getting serious.

A championship was four wins away. The one thing that could pro-pel my career farther than anything else was four wins away. The one thing that could almost guarantee me a contract over the summer was four wins away. A ring would stamp our team with that winner label— one that you never lose. Once again, we were faced with being on the road. This time, against a hot Portland Pirate team.

We traveled to Portland, Maine, in hopes of taking one of the first two games. Making the matchup even more interesting for me was the fact that my college roommate, Ken Klee, played for the Pirates. The championship series had everything that one could imagine. Each team was fighting for the chance to wear the ring. Every period, every shift, and every play carried the weight of being the deciding moment.

After two games in Portland, each team had managed to win one game. Going back to Moncton we felt like the series was under our con-trol. We had been the away team during our first two playoff series and managed to overcome the extra road game. Once again, we eked out a win in the other team's building. We also knew that winning a series took four wins not one, and anything could happen and probably would. After splitting Games 3 and 4, we headed into Game 5 thinking we needed to win in order to have a good chance heading back to Portland. Game 5 turned out to be the game that broke our backs. Each team bat-tled through what seemed like would never end. Regulation came and went and the first overtime came and went. Players no longer talked on the bench, trying to conserve what little energy they had left. We looked at each play as though it would decide the outcome of the game. One eventually did. Late in the second overtime, Portland silenced the Monc-ton crowd by sneaking the puck past our goalie.

Portland had come into Moncton and taken control of the series. In Games 3 and 4 we found ourselves battling it out with the one thing that can turn the tide in any hockey game—a hot goalie. They had one in Olaf Kolzig. Whatever we shot at him, including the water bottle, he turned it aside. In the two games we lost in Moncton to the Pirates, we outshot them 94 to 46. Although at the time none of us admitted it, heading back to Portland having to take the last two games in their building didn't leave us with much chance.

Early in the second period of Game 6, the Pirates built a two-goal lead and the spiritual life started to drain out of our physically spent bodies. The battles and injuries we had endured through the first three rounds caught up to us. The Pirates eventually overpowered us and won the Cup. I will never forgive them.

To sit in a locker room with a group of guys with whom you used all of your wits, expended every last bit of energy, and still lost was a memorable emotional experience. I had never been moved to tears by the game of hockey, but it didn't seem odd that grown men were weeping unabashedly. I had always been told that winning a championship and being on a winning team was something a person never forgets. But the guys that I played with in Moncton are some of the players I respect most in this game. We hadn't won a championship, but everyone battled and sacrificed through an unforgettable season and a playoff that almost finished with a storybook ending. I wonder if one thinks fondly about teammates because you enjoy the elation of winning, or if it is because of the hard work, struggles, and sacrifices that each member contributed. Does Joy or Struggle have the longer memory?

Having battled through a grueling playoff, having grown my first playoff beard, and having witnessed the sacrifice and pain that players were willing to put themselves through just to have a shot at winning a championship, I gained a new respect for the endurance, stamina, and determination it takes to win a ring. Looking back on that experience, I can only hope I get another chance to make a championship run. It would be nice if it were against Ken Klee. I owe him a loss in a championship series and he keeps reminding me of it with his ring.

After taking a few days to collect myself, it was time to have a year-end meeting with the Assistant General Manager of the Winnipeg Jets. They were interested in signing me to a contract and negotiations had gone as far as putting a three-year deal with a sizable signing bonus on paper. Winnipeg's Assistant GM even mentioned that they would probably sign me within the next month. The next day, that same Assistant GM was relieved of his duties and word came down that Winnipeg would not have their farm team in Moncton. As a result, Moncton would no longer have a team. It was rumored that Winnipeg would split their minor league players with Hartford, thus eliminating half of their farm system.

As if the loss of a place to play the next season wasn't bad enough, Lewis called with the devastating news that Winnipeg no longer had any interest in signing me for the coming year—let alone the three-year deal we had on the table. You tend to get ringing in your ears from kicks in the slats like that. I had finally made it to the AHL, finally proved that I could be a major contributor to a championship caliber team, and now they didn't even want to sign me. Many of my teammates had said they thought I might get called up at the end of the year and get in a few games—and now I was kicked to the curb without a contract. I was very upset, but I was closer than I had ever been to the NHL.

Lewis didn't seem to be as upset as I was. He insisted that having made it to the finals had enabled a lot of teams to see me play and he was sure that contract offers would come. I had heard Lewis talk about contracts that were sure to come a couple of times before and we had come up empty.

Mowing lawns back in Grand Haven gave me plenty of time to con- template what hockey had in store for me. Luckily, I didn't have to think about it too long. Contract talks *did* start with a number of teams and I came to believe what Lewis had said, that I would eventually get a con- tract with someone. Some of the teams that called were just AHL teams, but some were attached to NHL teams. Portland and Adirondack had contacted Lewis and were interested. Rob Laird, who no longer had a team to coach with the demise of Moncton, also called and asked me to keep my options open for a little while longer. He believed he was about to get a coaching job in the IHL and he wanted to take me with him.

Adirondack's interest was an NHL deal (which meant I would be part of the Detroit Red Wing organization and attend the parent team's training camp) with a possible signing bonus. Washington wasn't ready to make Portland's deal an NHL contract, so I eliminated Portland from the mix.

When Rob Laird finally got the job with the Phoenix Roadrunners of the IHL, the negotiations started to pick up. Phoenix made an offer totaling three years, forcing the Red Wings to make their offer for three years as well. The Phoenix deal wasn't an NHL contract and I desperately wanted a chance to work my way onto an NHL team. Lewis told Laird that if he could talk Phoenix's parent club, the L.A. Kings, into making the deal into an NHL contract, I would probably pick the Kings over the Red Wings. Although I had been a Red Wing fan my whole life and would have loved to put on the red and white of Detroit, I felt that Los Angeles offered a better situation in which to work my way into the NHL. Detroit seemed to be a team on the rise with a lot of young talent. L.A. had peaked, had started to age and was in need of fresh young talent. Also, the coach of their minor league team was someone I had just played for. I was sure Coach Laird would be a big backer of mine and that doesn't hurt when you're trying to impress people in the NHL.

The Kings agreed to the three-year deal and I jumped at the chance to sign my first NHL contract at age twenty-three. Not only did I finally have some security with a three-year deal, I had the chance to go to an NHL training camp with a contract in my hand. If I got sent down this time, coaches and management could no longer say, "We're sending you home because we don't have any contracts." For once, I was going to be one of the players that had a contract.

Oh yes, there was also going to be this guy at training camp named Wayne Gretzky. I was going to get a chance to play—or at least practice—with the "Great One."

5

THE KINGS

JAY

Dan was very excited about going to the Kings' training camp. He again spent the summer mowing lawns and worked out every day. Occasionally I would go to the Grand Haven YMCA to spot (assist) him in his weight training. Frankly, to see him squat lift 500 pounds and see the iron bar bend around his shoulders under that much weight scared me. I could envision the bar snapping and the weights collapsing and pinching Dan's legs off at the knees. He did weights four days a week, ran or biked one or two days, and walked more than ten miles a day mowing lawns. If he didn't make the Kings, it wouldn't be because he wasn't in condition.

That summer Dan and Mary Beth chaperoned another group of young people from Christ Community Church on a summer work trip, this time to Kentucky to help build homes for Habitat for Humanity.

Training camp didn't last as long as Dan had hoped. But he wasn't sent down before he got a chance to play on the same ice, do the same drills, and be on the same team with his childhood hockey idol—the Great One—Wayne Gretzky. He also was rewarded with the opportunity to play in a preseason exhibition game against the New York Rangers. It would be the first time in an NHL uniform. Nancy and I bought plane tickets to see the game. Early in the morning of our intended departure, Nancy's father passed away from a year-long illness.

We arranged for Dan to fly home for the funeral. Nancy's father had been the one who had inspired all those backyard ice rinks. He had been with the boys on their first fishing trips. He was the one who packed the Saturday morning "Grandpa's Brunch" for our six-some golf outings. I believe we can't know God. The only way we can experience Him is through the love of others and we had all experienced God's love through John Oole.

Scott suggested that his brothers and I steal away early on the morning of the funeral and go fishing at the lake where the Ooles had a small cottage when the boys were growing up. It would be a proper way to celebrate the life of someone who had meant so much to us.

On a given morning, if the five of us and Grandpa Oole had caught seven or eight bass between us, it would be noteworthy. That memorable morning, in just a few hours, we caught thirty bass and two Northern Pike. We sank Grandpa's well-worn fishing hat weighted down by one of his favorite lures in a tear-filled tribute to a wonderful father-in-law and grandfather. One of the bass was a lunker worthy to be mounted, and it now hangs in Dan's den. It was only fitting that Dan caught what was by far the biggest fish because, as Dan contended, "It was his (Grandpa's) way of showing beyond a shadow of a doubt who his favorite grandson was." The formal funeral service that followed was anticlimactic and unnecessary for the boys and me.

As the 1994/95 season began (the first year of Dan's three year contract with the Kings) I asked him what his goals were. They were clear in his mind: play the first year of the contract for Phoenix, split the second year with Phoenix and the Kings, and play the third year with the Kings. He would then be in position to sign an additional contract with the Kings.

As it turned out, that's almost the way it happened. He spent the entire first year in Phoenix, playing in 81 games with 19 goals and 23 assists. One of the highlights of the season for us was the Roadrunners' trip to nearby Kalamazoo to play the K-Wings. What started as getting tickets for the family and a few friends became a sixty-person entourage. Dan rewarded our efforts by scoring a few minutes into the game. The cheer for that goal was as loud as any for the K-Wings.

At season's end, Dan was awarded the Iron Man award for playing in every game. Actually, he had sat out only one game due to injuries in three professional seasons. This in a sport where there can be a lot of injuries.

Dan would often say they were playing with a shortened roster. So-and-so is out and so-and-so is hurting.

"The team seems to have a lot of injuries," I said to him once. "What's wrong with so-and-so?"

"Heart trouble."

"Heart trouble! Is it career-threatening?"

"It could be."

"What specifically is the problem?"

"Can't find a pulse."

It was Dan's way of saying that the player had an injury that he could have played with but he lacked the will to make the sacrifice. "Heart trouble"—being unwilling to suck it up and play over pain— was a condition Dan could not stomach.

The following summer Dan and Mary Beth were married in a beautiful ceremony in our home church. The dinner table got even more crowded when Greg married his fiancée a few weeks later. Not long after, Dan and Mary Beth chaperoned another group of young people from Christ Community Church and assisted Rev. Terry Troya in her work among the homeless in Staten Island, N.Y.

That same summer, Dan began to operate a hockey camp in Grand Rapids. His brother Jon, now a practicing attorney in Grand Rapids, incorporated the West Michigan Hockey Camp, Inc. Dan felt it was an opportunity to give something back to the area that gave him his start. Mary Beth, an all-conference gymnast from B.G., took charge of the off-ice training, teaching the kids plyometrics (an exercise regime that strengthens leg muscles and increases foot speed), the very same training techniques she puts Dan through in preparation for his seasons. Seventy-four kids from ages seven to eighteen attended the inaugural sessions. Dan's emphasis was on fun and fundamentals and on stressing that sports is a microcosm of life. I was featured in the camp as well, giving a talk to the parents entitled "So Your Son Wants to Play in the NHL?" Based on the feedback received from the campers and their parents, the camp was a success and Dan was encouraged to repeat the camp the next year.

Dan returned to the Kings' preseason training camp with high hopes. He had had a good year with Phoenix and this was the year his goals called for playing some games in the NHL. The Kings had a new coach in Larry Robinson who, it was reported, appreciated hard-working, gritty players. Dan was disappointed when he was sent down to Phoenix after only one week of the Kings' camp.

We made it a point to travel to the Roadrunner games that were within a reasonable driving distance. Reasonable driving distance is a relative term, but for us that meant Milwaukee, Chicago, Fort Wayne, Indianapolis, Kalamazoo, and Detroit. The Roadrunners were scheduled to play in Milwaukee against the Admirals on December 12, so I made arrangements to call on some customers while we were in the area. We stayed in the same hotel as the team and had dinner with Dan the evening before the game. The next morning, I left early to call on my customers. At one stop, after presenting my business card, the receptionist said, "Oh, Mr. Bylsma. Your wife phoned and left a message for you to call her as soon as possible."

Over thirty-five years of marriage, Nancy had never called me at the office of a customer. As I dialed our hotel, all I could think of was the worst about her aged mother and my ailing father.

"Nance, what is it?"

"We won't be seeing Daniel play the Admirals tonight," she replied.

"Why not? What's happened?" While my fears turned to the possibility of Dan sustaining an injury in practice or that he had became ill, there was a school-girl giddiness in her voice.

"He's been called up to the Kings. He's on his way to the airport as we speak."

My happiness over the news was not lost on the receptionist. "You look like you won the lottery," she said.

"Better than that," I said. "This is something that all the money in the lottery can't buy. My son got called up to play in the National Hockey League."

Scott called us that evening. "Was I right? All along I was right! I told you he would be in the NHL someday."

Dan played in two games before he was sent back to Phoenix, one against the Ottawa Senators and one against the Toronto Maple Leafs. When he called after each game, he could not contain his excitement. He had actually played on a line with Wayne Gretzky and Jari Kurri! He had taken a regular shift, he had played on the power play and penalty killing unit, and he sat next to Marty McSorley in the dressing room. And did I see him check Wendel Clark?!! Irrepressible joy and excitement tumbled out in sentence after breathless sentence.

"Will you be able to sleep?" I asked.

"Probably not."

"So tell me," I said, "what's the biggest difference between the show and the IHL?"

"You have to think faster," he reflected. "And there are other things: the goalies are better, the defensemen carry the puck better and skate better, and, of course, the overall talent is better. But the biggest thing is that you have to think faster."

"Can you play at this level?"

"Let's not kid ourselves," Dan said. "At my best, I'm not going to be a first line player. But I'll get better as I get more experience and confidence. Right now, all I think about when I'm on the ice is not making mistakes and *that's* a mistake. As I get acclimated, I'll feel more comfortable. But yes, I can play at this level."

After the two games, the injured player he had replaced healed, so Dan was sent back to Phoenix. But he had made it. For one brief shining moment, he had made it.

On February 6, he called at the usual time to tell us about the game that night and how he had played. It was 2:30 a.m. our time, 11:30 p.m. Phoenix time. He told us he'd been called up again. Two more times he got to play with Gretzky. During the second game, he started a two-on-one with Gretzky. When he turned to position himself to take Gretzky's pass and shoot, to his everlasting chagrin, he lost his edge and fell. He had a chance to score his first NHL goal on a pass from the Great One . . . and he fell.

One Los Angeles sports writer cited that incident as one of the reasons Gretzky wanted to be traded. I thought Dan had played well. Apparently, so did Coach Robinson because he told Dan after the game that he had done what they had asked of him, that he had proved he could play at the NHL level, and that they would probably call him back up over the weekend for the rest of the season.

Within a few days, Gretzky was traded to St. Louis for several forwards. That crowded the roster and Dan spent the rest of the season playing for Phoenix. Another disappointment. His play, however, did not go unnoticed by the Roadrunners. He had 22 goals and 20 assists. He was given the "C" (appointed captain) and was selected as the MVP for the Roadrunners for the season.

I thought he would repeat as the Iron Man because he had played every game for the Roadrunners except for when he was called up. But there was another, little-known reason I thought he would get it. Dan was skilled at blocking the shots that were taken from the blue line by the opposing players during their power plays. Absorbing one such shot broke his big toe during a game toward the end of the regular season.

Our 2:30 a.m. phone conversation that particular night went something like this:

"I saw you go down and then hobble to the bench in the third period, Dan. What happened?"

"The trainer thinks I broke my big toe. I need to have X-rays taken tomorrow."

"That's too bad. If it's broken, will you be out for the season?"

"No. If they can get the swelling down in time, I'll play tomorrow night."

"Doesn't it hurt?"

"I can't even walk on it. But the doctor will shoot me up with something and if I can get my foot in the boot (skate), I think I can play."

"You think you can play with a broken big toe that you can't walk on?"

"Walking is different than skating," Dan said. "The skate boot is like a cast; the foot is immobile. Don't worry, Dad, I won't do anything to injure myself."

"Sounds a little crazy to me," I said.

"We still need to get to the playoffs. Your toe is a long way from your heart. If it's at all possible, I have to play."

He played six games with that broken toe. When they shot him up with medication (it gives me shivers just to explain it), the team physician would insert a needle under the toenail and over the nail bed. The doctor would then *move* the tip of the needle to spread the painkilling medication around.

Nurse Mom had a question about the procedure. "Who's going to do the injection when you're on the road?"

"We can't ask the other team's doctor to do it," Dan told her, "because that will obviously tip them off that I'm injured. So the doctor taught me how to do it to myself."

Sure.

When he called after the next road game, Nancy was curious as to how the self-administered anesthetizing went.

Dan laughed. "I couldn't bring myself to do it," he said, "so I just played with the pain. The hard part was getting my foot into the boot. After that, it wasn't too bad."

Dan had a size eleven foot that he crammed—broken toe and all—into a size nine and a half skate. If something was going to keep him from playing full-time in the NHL, I knew it wouldn't be heart trouble.

The summer following his first call-up, he ran another successful hockey camp. One hundred and fifteen kids participated during the two weeks of camp. A lot of the kids were repeaters, coming back for another year of Mary Beth's plyometrics and Dan's Tennis Ball Warfare (campers had to dodge tennis balls being shot at them off the sticks of the instructors). The fundamentals of hockey and the fundamentals of life, now taught by a real, live NHLer. I was proud that they were such good role models—young adults that any kid could genuinely look up to and find some things that he could apply to his own life. Again the evaluations from the campers and their parents indicated that the program was finding solid support and should be continued.

Dan worked hard throughout the summer in anticipation of having a good training camp. He had showed them he could play at the NHL level and the Kings were on a youth movement. The big-name players had been traded. There appeared to be spots that could be won.

He survived the first two weeks of training camp and the first two cuts. Every time he called home I would ask the same question. "How are you doing?"

"I'm still here."

"I know you're still there. How are you doing?"

"I'm still here."

"Has anybody said anything to you? Any hint of your status?"

"The only thing I know for sure," he said, "is that I'm still here."

Exhibition games started and so did he. Dan didn't dress for the exhibition game in Phoenix against the Coyotes—this was the game in which some of the guys who had been sent down would get a chance to play. Then after the last exhibition game, the team was scheduled to go to a golfing resort in the mountains for a few days of rest and relaxation before the final week of practice. Before the trip, the assistant GM asked Dan if he had his clubs in Los Angeles. It seemed a clear signal that he was on the team, and some of the veteran players talked to him as if he had made the team, but his phone calls home were only guardedly optimistic. And rightly so.

There had been so many disappointments in the past. He had grasped the brass ring before, only to have it slip from his fingers. There were some injured players. If some hadn't recovered in time for the season opener, maybe, just maybe . . .

The morning of opening night, he called. "Dad, it's Daniel. I'm in the lineup."

We had bought a satellite dish when he was in Phoenix so we were able to watch the game and the opening night introductions. "From Grand Haven, Michigan," the PA announcer called, "number forty-two . . . right wing . . . Dan . . . Byyyyyyy-lsma." He drew out the "long i" sound of Bylsma as if it had caught in his throat and he couldn't get to the "uls-mah" part. I confess that as I saw Danny skating into streams of spotlight in the darkened Great Western Forum, the thought crossed my mind that this might be happening in my dreams. "Oh God," I prayed, "let this be real." Oh how I wanted it to be real. I wanted all of my encouragement to him, and my prayers for him, and all his dreams to be coming true. I wanted all the disappointments I had watched him weather and overcome to be swallowed up in the reality of this one bright shining moment in this ice palace of Camelot—and they were.

Over the next few weeks, Dan's attitude was to take it shift by shift, game by game, week by week. One of his sayings, those snacks for the soul he was fond of quoting, was, "No one is promised tomorrow, so do what you can today." That statement is so true in professional athletics, where an injury, a general manager's whim, a trade, or a careless mistake can cost someone a career. So, game in and game out, Dan worked hard and played as if the game he was playing in *was* his opportunity. It was one game at a time for the entire season.

I thought he played well, well enough to be a solid member of the team. But he never once took his place for granted. With just a few games left in the season, he would still call after the morning skate on game day and repeat the words he uttered the first game of the season, "Dad? Daniel. I'm in the lineup."

Just before Christmas, he called and we had an easy conversation. His tone was casual and he sounded relaxed—at ease with his situation for a change. I mentioned it. He responded, "Whether I play another game in the NHL or not just doesn't matter. Some other of the Kings and I visited the Los Angeles Children's Hospital yesterday to play Santa Claus. I was assigned to the cancer ward. I saw death in the eyes of a twelve-year-old child. Here I am worrying if I'm in the lineup tomorrow and this little kid doesn't even know if tomorrow will come. It puts things into perspective rather quickly."

Even though he only scored three goals and had six assists in 79 games, others saw what I was seeing through a father's eyes.

"Bylsma made his mark the old-fashioned way—through hard work. He was a valued penalty killer on one of the best units in the NHL and was doing what every coach loves—going into the corners and grinding it out." The Hockey News *11/5/96*

"He (Bylsma) is one of the best, if not the best, shot blocker penalty killers in the NHL." Larry Robinson, L.A. Kings coach

"The Kings have not had many bright spots this season; one of them is the penalty killing unit which has been among the top three in the NHL all season long. The reason, Dan Bylsma is the first one over the boards to kill penalties. He's one of the best shot- blockers in the league and consistently makes intelligent decisions under pressure." Jim Fox, Fox Sports West sportscaster for the Kings' telecasts

"L.A. KINGS - OVERACHIEVER Left Winger Dan Bylsma showed tireless determination on the league's third-ranked penalty killing unit." The Hockey News *5/2/97*

The Kings' penalty killing unit set a team record of 87.2% efficiency in the 1996/1997 season, a percentage which ranks fifth best all-time in the NHL record book. At the end of the 1996/1997 season, Dan was voted "Most Popular Player" by the Kings Booster Club, an honor he shared with penalty killing linemate and good friend Ian "Lappy" Laperriere, and he was the recipient of the Kings' "Community Service Award" which he shared with goalkeeper Byron Dafoe.

The Phoenix Roadrunners announced they were ceasing operations as of the end of the 1996/1997 season. They also announced the selection of Dan to the All-Time Best Phoenix Roadrunner Team. Dan's reaction? "They must have picked four full lines."

So your son wants to play in the NHL? Prepare him for life. Dan's press clippings and awards do not say he was flashy or dazzling or talented. They recognize his hard work, his intelligence, his tireless determination, his character, his citizenship. These are things over which Dan had control. These traits are products of his environment. These are characteristics that helped Dan overcome the disappointments over the selection process at the Michigan Midget Camp, the difficulties with his first GM, the relegation to the third line and penalty killing in college, the disappointments of his first training camp in Moncton, the handshake and "don't forget your hat" from the Mighty Ducks' inaugural training camp, Moncton's later collapse, and the interminable years in the minor leagues. These are also the characteristics that will help Dan achieve success in life after hockey or any other goal for which he dreams. For nearly every player, *life after hockey* comes sooner rather than later.

DAN

My contract with the Kings forced me to set new goals for myself and my career. I thought that playing out the first year of my contract in Phoenix, splitting the second year between Phoenix and Los Angeles, and playing the third year for L.A. would be a realistic goal . . . and a dream come true.

Thoughts of making a good impression at training camp motivated me to work as hard as I ever have in the summer. The guaranteed contract over the next three years gave me the financial security I needed to dedicate more time than ever to training for camp. It also gave me the opportunity to buy a ring for the girl I met in that freshman geography class at Bowling Green. Mary Beth graciously accepted my marriage proposal and we began planning our wedding for the summer of 1995.

As training camp neared, I focused on making a good impression. I realized that the chance of going to L. A. and making the team was one in a million, but I knew I had an opportunity to make a positive impression during camp. L. A. signed me solely on Rob Laird's recommendation. In fact, no one in the organization had seen me play and I wasn't on anyone's list of people to watch at camp. Knowing that, my goal was to leave a good impression on the coaching staff before I headed to Phoenix at the start of the season. On the first day of training camp with the Kings, everyone arrived at the hotel for physical exams and various strength tests. Not knowing many people, I kept to myself. I had just gotten in line to see the eye doctor when a nearby door opened and out popped Wayne Gretzky. He exchanged niceties with some of the players waiting in line in front of me as I stared in awe. Before walking on to his next testing site he stopped, held out his hand and said, "Hi, I'm Wayne Gretzky."

No kidding! If there was some brilliant reply to be made, it escaped me and all I could manage was to blurt out something that only faintly resembled "Dan Bylsma." The man who didn't need any introduction had introduced himself to *me*.

The first time I was on the ice with him, I thought: *Wow. I'm out here for the same reason he is!* What was really interesting though, was that during practice not many of the young draft picks and newcomers were brave enough to get in line to do a drill with him. Although I understood why, I still wanted the chance to say "I was on a two-on-one with Wayne Gretzky." (Little did I know what a curse that could be.) Believe me, it was downright intimidating to be on the ice with arguably the greatest player ever to play the game. I didn't want to do a drill with him and mess it up, but at the same time I wanted to get a chance to play with him even if it was in practice.

Camp went well. The physical testing had me near the top of camp for fitness but, as players often noted, "A dumbbell never scored a goal," and "It's tough to translate 75 push-ups into X number of goals." After practicing a few days, players were divided into three teams for a round robin tournament. The two best teams played a championship game to determine a winner, and then we had a full scrimmage for the fans. In total, I played four games and I was pleased with the results. I had five points in four games, the third most in camp and more importantly (in my mind anyway) I tied with Gretzky. I'd like to tell you that he got his five points by going all out. In training camp? What do you think?

Overall, training camp had gone just about as I had planned and I was hopeful that I would get a shot at an exhibition game. First cuts were to come before the exhibition games and I could only hope that my performance in the first week of camp had at least earned me a few extra days. It didn't. Getting called into the office to see the GM is rarely a good thing, especially in training camp. I was informed that I had a good camp and was scheduled to play in an exhibition game against the New York Rangers, but I was getting sent to Phoenix. I was disappointed that I hadn't made it past the first cut, but I had accomplished what I had set out to do—make a good impression. I had hoped that I would get a chance to play in an exhibition game and I was getting one. I was going to play against a real NHL team.

Playing against the Rangers proved two things to me: I was capable of handling myself at that level, but I still needed to improve before I was ready to play there full-time.

We began the season in Phoenix hoping we'd have a strong team, one that would compete for a top spot in the league. Things didn't work out according to plan. The team didn't take to Rob Laird's coaching style and a number of our best players fell out of favor with the coach. I, on the other hand, was one of the players Rob Laird had brought in and was "one of his boys." It took much of the season to pull together a group of guys who were willing to play for "Robo." It also took some time for me to gain the respect of my teammates, perhaps because I was viewed as one of the coach's favorites.

As a team we never seemed to be able to get a cohesiveness and, as a result, winning never came easy. We made it to the second round of the playoffs but our team never lived up to its potential during the regular season or the playoffs. It was a disappointing year from the standpoint of what our team was or wasn't able to accomplish.

For the first part of the season we were distracted, protesting a coaching style that was not to the team's liking. Many players were traded and others never got the playing time they thought they deserved. As a group, we couldn't accept the coach's plan for the team. As a result, doing what the coach asked of you and doing extra work became something that was discouraged by the team as a whole. I had trouble understanding how the team could foster a culture that would discourage individuals from trying to improve themselves into becoming better players. We all wanted to win, didn't we? We all wanted to move on to the NHL, didn't we? How could a conflict with a coach turn a team against the two things that we played the game for?

Personally, I felt I was improving and becoming a better all-around player. Penalty killing had become a huge part of my value to the team. My scoring touch was never a strong point of my game since I became a defensive forward, but I was able to find the net enough times to finish the year as the fifth leading scorer on the team with 19 goals and 23 assists in 82 games.

Reflecting back on my first year in the Kings' organization, I had accomplished most of the goals that I had set for myself. Training camp had gone well and I was sure that I had given management some positive signs about my ability. I had stepped into a new league, the IHL, and proved that I could be a contributor. My goal of playing in at least one NHL regular season game didn't happen, but I was convinced that I had made some headway in my career. As summer began, I was convinced that I was closer to making the NHL than ever.

With that as my motivation, I set out to make sure that I would be in even better shape for the next training camp. I knew a good summer would give me a chance to earn some games with the Kings. The Kings hired a new coach during the summer and his promise of demanding a hard work ethic gave me some hope that this might be the year. I had nothing if not a hard work ethic.

Heading out to Los Angeles that year, I felt as confident as I ever had, entering a training camp. Not because I thought I had a chance at making the team, but because I had been through the experience the previous year. I knew what was going to be expected of us and what the practices and scrimmages would be like. I knew most of the guys and felt comfortable talking with most of the people in the organization. I was hoping that would settle me down a little and allow me to have an impressive camp.

Unfortunately, camp didn't last long. Even though I tested well and put up points in the scrimmages, I was called in for the first round of cuts. I was extremely disappointed and upset when they broke the news that I was going down. It was the second year of my three-year contract—the year I felt I had to play in some NHL games. At every other level in hockey, I had been the youngest. Now I was twenty-five years old, very late to start an NHL career. My biological clock was ticking. I had to come to grips with the fact that I didn't even make the second week of camp. While I had the security of knowing I would be playing in the IHL, my dreams of playing in the NHL began to have less luster.

I didn't know when the Kings might call someone up or if they would ever need to call someone, but I was going to be ready. I was going to work myself into a position to be the person they would call up.

The call came on December 12 as I was walking out of my hotel room in Milwaukee. I was on my way to have breakfast with my mother so I expected that she would be on the line when I picked up the phone. Instead, it was Coach Laird with "the call." My heart was racing and my mind was a jumble as I scrambled to calm myself and get all the necessary information. I was to get on an airplane bound for Los Angeles at 1:28 p.m. I was a Los Angeles King!

My seemingly unattainable dream was a reality. I was going to dress in the same locker room, sit on the same players' bench, and play on the same team as Wayne Gretzky—in the National Hockey League. I didn't know how I was going to sleep that night. I called Mary Beth and asked her to fly in and share this incredible moment with me.

My mom was just as excited as I was but she was still my mom. Did I have clean underwear? Did I have enough dress shirts? Was that the only tie I was packing? Thinking I needed more stuff, she went off to a department store while I tried to eat breakfast. Breakfast, however, was like a quiz show where the category was "First Game in the NHL." Where were we going to be playing? Who would be Dan Bylsma's first opponent in his first official game? How was I going to get to the rink? What was it going to be like in the locker room with all those NHL greats?

My mind raced from what it might be like to score in my first game, to our backyard where I scored so many NHL goals in my head, to wondering how long I would stay a King, to how long I had been working to get to that moment. It was such a rush that I don't remember any of the details of the airplane ride. At one point, I thought to myself that if I could bottle the excitement that I was feeling I could put the Cedar Point Amusement Park out of business.

The call-up to L.A. lasted for two games and then I was sent back to Phoenix. In February, I was called up again for two more games. Only four games . . . but I had finally made it to the "Show" and it was better than my dreams. It made me even more determined to do what I had to do to get back there and stay there.

The summer of 1996 had come and gone and training camp was upon us again. It was clear this was going to be a make or break year for me. I was entering the last year of my three-year contract and I was turning 26 on the nineteenth of September. My career timeline was beginning to edge toward its midpoint. Not many players break into the NHL after they turn 25, let alone 26. I needed to play enough games that season in order to impress a team—any team—enough to give me another NHL contract. I had set a goal of playing at least 25 games in the show. I had a lurking suspicion that I might be setting my goal a little high but I also felt it was better to aim too high than too low.

Training camp started just like every other training camp for me. The first week was primarily filled with physical testing and scrimmaging, with the first cut coming at the end of the week. Things had gone well in the testing and I had been able to get on the scoreboard in the scrimmages with a goal and three assists in four intrasquad games. As the first week wore on and the first cuts loomed, it appeared the Kings had gotten younger over the summer and that there were more opportunities for new players to make an impression.

Rumors always floated around as to when cuts would come, but usually it happened the day before the first exhibition game. That day came and went and something strange happened that I had never experienced—nothing. I had no meeting with management; better yet, my name appeared on the list for the players to play in the first exhibition game.

I was in uncharted waters. I had hoped, even expected, to make it this far, but I wasn't quite sure how it would feel or how I would react. It didn't have the satisfaction I thought it would have; the angst just became greater. Now there was a whole new series of questions and uncertainties lying around the next turn. How many exhibition games would I get? When was the next cut going to be? What did it mean that I was playing on this line or that line?

"Control what you can control and be ready," rang in my ears yet again. Hadn't I heard those same words at every turn?

Exhibition games started and the Kings played well. It was tough to get a reading on how I was doing, but I felt I was hanging in there, even taking care of business a time or two. I played in all the exhibition games so far and I wondered what that meant. Had I been playing well enough to merit additional games? Two cuts had come and gone; when would the next one be?

My confidence was increasing and I was beginning to prove, at least to myself, that I could play at this level. I got a goal and an assist and was +3 in the first four games I had played. I hoped that I was convincing the people around me as well. The Kings had won all their exhibition games and there was a good feeling surrounding the team. I just hoped that this meant good things for Dan Bylsma.

As training camp progressed, it looked more and more as if it was coming down to a few other players and me. NHL rules allow for a 24-man roster. To the best of my psychic powers, I figured I was somewhere between 22nd and 26th and, believe me, I ran just about every scenario one could imagine. Everything was a new experience for me. The pressure mounted as the end of training camp drew near. The amount of unanswerable questions you can ponder in your hotel room are limitless and cannot be anticipated. Riding in chartered planes, staying in the best hotels, and the choices at the pregame meals were experiences I could not have imagined and I wanted it all to continue.

With the start of the season just a few days away, the Kings' management took the team to a resort in the mountains in order to get some quality practice time away from the distractions of Los Angeles and to bring us closer together as a team. The Assistant General Manager, Dave Taylor, asked me if I had a set of golf clubs in L.A. or if I needed a rental set. I could only assume that meant I was going to the resort with the team, not back to the golf capital of the world and the home of the Phoenix Roadrunners. I can remember the series of phone calls I made to Mary Beth, my parents, and the rest of my family when I learned I was going on that trip. But ... I still had to survive the last cut. And the last cut is the cruelest cut of all.

As the first game neared, another strange thing happened—nothing. If I survived, I had expected someone to come and tell me that I was going to be starting the year with the Kings. But it never happened. Two days before the start of the season, the final two individuals were sent down and I was with the team, practicing, getting ready for the start of the season. I didn't know if I was going to be playing in the first game or not.

My parents had as many questions as I didn't have answers. My dad said, "What do you mean, you don't know if you're going to be in the lineup?"

"I guess I'll find out tomorrow at the pregame skate," I told him. I really didn't know.

Sure enough, the next morning at the pregame skate the lines were posted for that night's game and I had made the lineup.

I couldn't believe what was happening. Not only had I made the team, I was playing in the first game. Coming into training camp, I had hoped to have a shot at gaining a spot on the team but I wouldn't have given very good odds on it happening. Now here I was on the verge of *starting* the first game. But the pressure I felt and the questions I'd been asking the walls of the hotel room didn't stop. A few players were injured and one, or possibly two, players would be sent down when everyone was healthy. So I still wasn't sleeping soundly.

Mary Beth came to visit me in training camp from Phoenix where she had been staying with a high school friend's family. It had given her a chance to start her job at Bally's as a personal trainer. It was an awkward situation for the two of us, but NHL teams aren't required to provide lodging for wives or family. Staying back home in Michigan would have kept us too far apart and, simply stated, we had to plan around the possibility I would be starting the season in Phoenix.

Away from the rink, my mind was at full speed. But at the rink, the NHL was everything dreams are made of. The packed arenas, games on television, highlights on ESPN, and playing beside stars like Wayne Gretzky and Mario Lemieux. The media and interviewers were at the rink every day, although it wasn't me they were crowding around. It seemed that the world was at our feet. Television and movie stars showed up to watch our games. I had paid for many a movie ticket to see Kurt Russell or Goldie Hawn, but now they were coming to see *my* show.

Getting into Universal Studios, attending "The Tonight Show" or watching a taping of "Coach" and meeting some of the cast after the show were all just a phone call away. It was hard getting used to the fact that people saw us as stars or celebrities. I guess you *can* fool some of the people some of the time.

After a short home stand, we went on a three-game road trip to Montreal, Philadelphia, and Washington. I was going to get a chance to play in the hallowed home of the Montreal Canadiens and on Broad Street in Philly, an opportunity that my parents could hardly pass up. They had never seen me play in the NHL and I still wasn't sure how long I was going to last with the Kings, so they packed their bags and headed to Montreal.

If there is a city where hockey is more a religion than a sport, it is Montreal. And no team has more tradition coursing through its past and present than the Montreal Canadiens. Two games into my first season with the Kings, I was going to play my first road game in Montreal's Molson Centre. Not only was I getting a chance to play in the Mecca of hockey, my parents had driven eighteen hours to see #42 for the first time live and in action. Since I had played in the first two games and had been on one of the top four lines in practice, I was confident my parents would get to see me on the ice and not in the stands.

Going through my pregame routine I was getting anxious about whether I was going to be in the lineup, but I tried to prepare as if I was. Before stretching out, we go for a light spin on the stationary bike to get the muscles loosened up. Riding the bike, I was telling my linemate and penalty killing partner, Ian Laperriere, how tonight's game would be the first that my parents had ever seen me play. The coach, Larry Robinson, overheard our conversation and approached the bikes.

"Disco," he said, using my nickname, "the coaching staff decided that we'd give one of the guys that had been sitting a chance to get in the game tonight. Is that going to be all right with you?"

Ian immediately dropped his head, not wanting to be a part of the conversation. "If you're asking if it's all right with me," I said, "no, it's not. But if you're telling me I'm out, I guess I'm out."

After a moment of awkward silence a big grin swept over Coach Robinson's face. "I overheard your conversation about your parents traveling from Michigan to see you play," he said. "I'm joking—you're in." Real funny, Larry.

After seeing the games in Montreal, Philadelphia, and Washington, my parents traveled to the Chicago and Detroit games as well. All the guys were beginning give me a hard time about the traveling Bylsma show, even the media picked up on the act and made reference to the fact that my mom and dad had been a mainstay on all the road games to date.

Even though I was beginning to settle into my role on the team, players were still injured and I knew there would be one or two senddowns when everyone was healthy. I had established myself on the penalty killing unit and was becoming confident that I could play in any defensive situation. I had played in every game to that point, but there were still a lot of unanswered questions running through my head. Mary Beth had to learn not to try to reduce my worries; eventually my mind would tire itself out and I would be able to relax. In training camp I was just hoping to make the team. Now I was hoping that the days turned into a week, and that I would still be there to get my first two-week paycheck. On November 1, I could hardly believe that I had been in the NHL a whole month.

It started out with my thinking that I would give anything for just one week in "the show," and before I knew it, I was ready to offer just about anything for another month. Soon I was hoping to be around at Christmas, then New Year's, and then staying until the end of the season seemed possible.

Hockey had become an unbelievable experience for me. In every game I played against someone whose hockey card I collected when I was a little boy. Now I was getting a chance to shut them down on their power play. Only by pinching myself on a regular basis could I keep myself in the real world and not in the dreams of my childhood.

It would seem that once you've reached the highest level in the world, the skill level of the individuals would be relatively close. But it is clearly apparent to most of the players in the NHL who the star players are and just how talented they are, even when compared to the rest of the league.

In a home game against the Pittsburgh Penguins, Jaromir Jagr put on a display that awed even our best players. He out-muscled one of our forwards for the puck and exploded by one defenseman into the neutral zone, creating a two-on-one with another Penguin against our other defenseman. As they neared our goalie, our defenseman played the two-on-one correctly by giving the goalie the shot and taking away the pass to their other offensive player. Jagr faked the pass, held onto the puck, and waited for the goalie to make the first move. When the goalie committed himself—and suddenly looked more like a fish out of water than a goalie—Jagr was left standing at the side of the net with not much more than a chip shot into the open cage. One of my teammates, Ray Ferraro, turned to me with his mouth open. "Was that any good?" he asked. Ferraro, arguably one of the Kings' best players, was in awe of the talent of another player in the league. I was glad to see I wasn't the only one.

As a new player in the league, it was easy to be in awe of the players, the arenas, the fans, the charter planes, the fancy hotels, and the big cities that were all a part of "the show." Part of the battle of staying focused on hockey was because of the glitter and glamour both on and off the ice. Knowing who to talk to, where to go, and what is appropriate is an important factor when trying to settle into the social atmosphere of the team. Even more important is being able to relax and concentrate on playing your best hockey every game. The problem is compounded when you are a young player or a rookie because many of the veterans have formed friendships and tend to stick together. And if you manage to do things to put you in disfavor, they can ruin you.

For example, say you are a high draft pick and come to camp as a rookie full of self-importance and cash in your pocket and show little respect for journeymen players whose names you don't recognize. Those veterans can make your life miserable and worse. The rookie knows the importance of making a good impression during practice. He is second in line to do a drill and a veteran is in front of him. Instead of taking off to take a pass and do the drill when his turn comes, the veteran skates to the rear of the line and leaves the rookie (who was not expecting it to be his turn) standing there like a dummy. The whistle blows, the drill comes to a stop, the rink becomes quiet, and the coach gets in the rookie's face for screwing up the drill. Little things done to fracture an inflated ego can also deflate a career.

I cannot stress enough how important it is have your head screwed on straight. The pressures one needs to handle at that level—uncertain career considerations, media relations, fan adulation, peer pressure, the pressure to perform, slumps in your performance, the inability to sense your place in the order of things, and yes, the lack of social graces—all of these have stymied many careers.

So your son wants to play in the NHL? Prepare him for life.

JAY

The hockey camp we held in the summer of 1997 had 130 participants, ranging in age from six to fifty-five. Again, the evaluations rated it as "the best camp I have ever attended" and indicated that our philosophy that sports is a microcosm of life was appreciated by the parents as much as Tennis Ball Warfare was appreciated by the participants. One evaluation stated: "What stands out with your camp is how you stress the total person. Thanks for a great week." Another parent wrote, "A totally awesome learning experience for my son. Thanks for taking your responsibility as a role model seriously." Someone else said, "I could tell you genuinely love the kids. You made a lasting impression on (my son)." We were pleased by the response and encouraged to expand the camp for the next year.

We drove Dan and Mary Beth to the airport to see them off to Los Angeles for the 1997/1998 season. I don't remember Dan showing as much anxiety over the start of any previous season as he showed for the start of this one. During the summer, he had trained as hard as he ever had. He said he was never more prepared. There had been three-a-day workouts and he had skated more than he ever had. But he was anxious, and in spite of his efforts to put on his "game face," the anxiety showed.

Perhaps it was because Mary Beth was four months pregnant and life had become less of a game and more of the serious stuff that fills up our adulthood all too quickly. Perhaps it was because he had tasted a season of success and didn't want to be disappointed again by not being in "the show."

More likely his anxiety was because the Kings had made a trade the previous week, sending Dmitri Khristich (a forward) and Byron Dafoe (a goalie who, with Byron's wife Kim, were among Dan and Mary Beth's best friends) to the Boston Bruins for two forwards. Before the trade, Dan felt that he was somewhere between the tenth and sixteenth forward, with fourteen of them to be on the team. Now he was among the tenth to the seventeenth and it meant the odds for making the team were now five out of eight instead of five out of seven. As he had said, it reminded him that it was that time of the year again—training camp. He had never attended one where he was certain of the outcome.

As we waited for the flight to be called, I wished there was something I could say, something I could do to assuage his angst. At times like those, there isn't much to be said, but the father in me felt the need to try. "You'll do just fine."

His reply was agitated, "I know I'll do better than fine. What I don't know is if it will be enough. It may be that the decision has already been made and there's nothing I will be able to do. What I can't do is let the uncertainty have a negative effect on my performance at camp. One of the factors that will determine who will make the team is how they are able to handle this pressure."

I realized that there were a lot of things that should be said. Not now . . . now was both too late and inappropriate. The time for saying them was when it had a shaping influence on this life for which I had a responsibility to raise. And I had said some of these things, things like, "You can't do anything about the things over which you have no control and you can't worry about those things. You can affect the things over which you have control; those are the things you need to work on."

I hugged him at the gate, wished him luck, and simply said the words I don't think a parent can say often enough, "I love you and I'm proud of you."

As Nancy and I walked to our car, we observed that this is a part of professional sports that very few people know. On every team there are several million-dollar players for whom training camp is a place to get in shape for the season. Then there is a group of middling players who have proved their worth in the past and have a reasonable comfort level that, barring injury or something else unforeseen, will have a regular role to play on the team. Then there is a group of players (in an NHL organization, about ten to fifteen) who, like Dan, need to fight for their spot every year, every game, every shift on the ice. They don't know if they will be able to grab the brass ring, and if so, for how long, or whether the brass ring will grab them. Frequently, they don't know where they will live or with whom or for how long.

By a workman's standard, they are paid huge salaries ($200,000 to $400,000 per year). But it's a mere fraction of the multimillion dollar contracts of some of the players they will play with. And every year, they board a plane bound for a training camp in some big city wondering if they'll make it, be sent back to the minors, or sent home.

For most of these players there is a family that is hoping and praying that the dream their child or husband holds will become a reality, not wanting him to feel the agony of disappointment, the pain of falling just a bit short of a stratospheric goal. There is the hope that the life lessons taught years before were absorbed and were enough. Enough to assist him if he makes it, and sustain him if he doesn't. There is also the knowledge that the decisions that affect the dreamer are often subjective, made on a whim, turned on an injury, and possibly simply a matter of time and place—factors over which the dreamer has no control. As a family member, this vicarious experience comes with an anxious excitement that goes through your whole being, a feeling with which you have a love/hate relationship. Love, for the child or husband to have the chance to make it; hate, for the real possibility that he will be disappointed yet another time. You wish there was something you could do but you know it's too late—far too late.

Danny, Danny. What will become of you?

Our conversations with Dan during the training camp were the same as before.

We would ask: "How is it going?"

He would answer: "I'm still here."

───────

In the exhibition game the day before the final cuts were to be made, he scored a goal and had an assist and thought he had played well. The next night he called to ask if the Long Beach Ice Dogs (of the IHL) played in Grand Rapids.

"You got sent down?"

"I got sent down."

"What did they say?"

"I got the usual nice words of consolation," he said. "'You had a good camp. You're the kind of player we are trying to develop here.

It wasn't anything you did. It's a numbers game. Don't be discouraged, you're only a phone call away. Anything can happen.' None of it makes me feel any better. I still got the boot. The hard part is not getting the boot, it's getting the boot instead of some of the players who didn't."

There's nothing a parent can say at that time to make it any better and a lot that can be said that will make it worse. We could only hope that this was yet another disappointment that he would take in stride, learn from, and use as a way to become a better person and a better hockey player. Playing for the Long Beach Ice Dogs, after all, was another opportunity disguised as a disappointment.

The day's transaction notices that reported that Dan had been sent down also carried the notice that Brendan Morrison, last year's Hobey Baker award winner—the best player in college hockey—had been sent down from New Jersey to their farm club. It was yet another reminder of the rarefied atmosphere in which Dan was trying to breath and survive.

It's October 13, 1997, and both the Kings and the Ice Dogs have played seven games. The Kings have won only one game; the Dogs are at 4-3. Dan is playing with a broken finger. The Kings have allowed six goals while killing 27 penalties for a 77.7% penalty killing efficiency, a big decline from their record-setting 87.7% the previous season. The Ice Dogs have allowed five goals in 54 short-handed situations for a 90.7% penalty killing efficiency, up from their percentage last season of 84.4%. I think the difference is Dan. So does the front office of the Ice Dogs. I can't help but wonder if anyone in the Kings' organization is noticing.

Three days later, someone noticed. Dan has been called up and is a Los Angeles King again. For how long, I don't know. What a roller coaster!

On October17th, he called to say he was in the lineup for that night's game with the Philadelphia Flyers.

I asked him, "Do they know your finger is broken?"

"Yes, they know," he said. It was answered in such a way that

Nancy and I are not sure that the Kings know there is a 40% displacement.

"What about your cast? Did you wear it to the rink?"

"No."

"Did you tell them about your hip pointer?"

"This is no time for heart trouble," he said.

We watched the game on the satellite. He was back at his old role, fourth-line mucker and first-line penalty killer. His dogged determination forces a turnover right at the end of the second period and it results in a goal that increases the Kings' lead to 4–1. Dan gets the assist and the Kings go on to beat the Flyers 5–1. I felt he played very well.

At 3:49 a.m. on the 18th, the phone rings. At first, the ringing fits into my dreams but then jars me out of a deep sleep. It is Dan. He was pleased with how the game went, thought he played well. He wanted to know what we thought. He was even more pleased with a private conversation he had with Coach Robinson as he was icing down his hip after the game. Dan's back with the Kings and it appears to be as permanent as these things can be. He is calling from his bed and he relates he can feel his unborn child move in Mary Beth's womb. The little bugger is very active at that moment. I suggest that it shares its father's unmistakable happiness.

One week later, the Kings lose to the Detroit Red Wings 4–1. Dan is now on the third line with his good friend and penalty killing partner Ian Laperriere. Dan set up Rob Blake to assist on the Kings' only goal. It's his second assist in four games. He continues to play well. The Red Wings' vaunted power play does not score against him when he and Lappy are killing the penalties.

On November 4th, Nancy and I travel to New Jersey to see the Kings play the Devils and do some research for this book. We have a quiet dinner with Dan. Precious quality time with each other, of which we have precious little. We discuss the child that has become obvious in Mary Beth's abdomen. We review the hockey camp brochure for the next season. Dan is struck by the size of his first paycheck under this contract and expresses the hope for fifteen more of them. We talk about how the team is doing and the dynamics of its current composition. Mom and Dad and kid stuff. Although we're in a strange place, it is the familiar family dinner table again and it is good. The Kings shut out the Devils 3–0 and the Devils' vaunted power play does not score in seven attempts. Dan plays very well. For the zillionth time, I lean over to Nancy during the game and say, "The player wearing #42 bears a remarkable resemblance to our son Daniel."

For the zillionth time she responds, "Really? You think so? I hadn't noticed. #42 for which team?" After ninety games over three seasons, we still can't believe we have a son who plays in the National Hockey League.

In the November 11 edition of the *L.A. Times* there was a very complimentary feature article about Dan by one of its sports editors, Bill Plaschke, entitled, "Not the Best, Only the Finest." The article and its title captures the essence of Dan's hard work, his character and his role as a lesser-light, but important, journeyman member of the Kings. Someone else understands that character matters. I'm very pleased that others see Dan as I do—that my fatherly eyes have not deceived me. Perhaps without meaning to, Plaschke pays a high compliment to Nancy and me and Dan's siblings. I am a proud father.

A few days later, Dan plays in the annual Kings Charity Golf Outing, an event where fans pay exorbitant greens fees to tee-it-up with a player and thereby raise money for charity. He calls to say he was in a foursome with Phil Anschutz, the owner of the Kings, and actors Alan Thicke (of the TV show "Growing Pains") and James Garner (of "Maverick" and "The Rockford Files"). A rarefied atmosphere in which he became at ease only after the shock of who his playing companions were wore off, and because they made him feel comfortable. He had a grand time. He remarked that this is one celebrity golf tournament where *he* will be the one who treasures the group picture—they probably pitched theirs. He told us that after he figured out how to swing the club with his broken finger, he played well and led the team to 15 under par and a second place finish.

Do sports help you in life? I don't believe Dan would have been invited into this select group if he were not an accomplished golfer. Will it get him anything? Who knows? But he had a great time, a unique and life-enriching experience for one day. If, as I suspect, the richness of one's life is measured by the texture of one's memories, this was a Persian rug day.

On December 5, Dan calls from Toronto to say that a sports columnist writing in an Ottawa, Ontario, newspaper had referred to him in a column. Not about his role in the game with the Ottawa Senators but about the time he fell down taking a pass from Wayne Gretzky on a two-on-one breakaway. The writer had used the incident as an example of rising to success in spite of an embarrassing fall. "I'm amazed," Dan said. "First, that anyone would even know about that incident, but also that they would remember my name in connection with it and that I still play in the NHL."

"Not many people are mentioned in the same breath as Wayne Gretzky," I said. "You're famous. If you had scored, the sporting world would have forgotten about it."

"I wish I could be remembered for something other than falling down on a two-on-one with Gretzky."

"That's *not* what you are remembered for," I said. "You're remembered for putting the fall behind you and becoming successful. Success is not in never falling, but in rising every time you fall."

New Year's Eve. Dan is still with the Kings, still takes a regular shift, still kills penalties. He is counting. Twenty-six days until their child is born, four more games before his contract goes one way (major league salary, whether he plays in the show or the minor leagues). He has one goal and five assists in twenty-six games; ahead of his three goals and six assists last year in seventy-eight games. He is still L.A.'s best penalty killer (statistically). He still takes every game as a gift. He still works hard every shift. He's loving life.

DAN

Journal Entry - September 5, 1997. *The month of September is the longest month of the year. Training camps open and players report to their teams. It's a time of indecision and uncertainty. Players battle for positions that may or may not be available and for contracts that may or may not ever be signed. Idle time is filled with questions that may never be answered.*

I feel as though I'm in line for a scary roller coaster ride. I've been on this thrill ride before. There's no other ride I'd rather be getting on, but each time I get ready to strap myself in it seems like a new situation, new circumstances with new possibilities and additional pitfalls.

I've prepared myself to the best of my ability, yet the ups and downs of the roller coaster ahead seem more frightening than ever. I'm not sure what's in store for me and I'm apprehensive. Once again my mind races over the possibilities, and my heart is a quite noticeable lump in my stomach.

What can I do to assure my future? How much of the outcome is truly in my control? Has it already been decided? Is it my job to take, or my job to lose?

I can envision every possible outcome, good and bad. I can envision each one a little differently an infinite amount of times. Daily.

Are the coaches watching? What are they looking for? Did the fact that I came in with some of the best scores in the off-ice testing matter at all? When the coach talked to me today, did that mean anything? Did the makeup of the line I skated on today mean anything?

I'm playing at least as well as some of the players with one-way contracts (contracts that generally assure they won't be sent to the minor leagues). Aren't I?

Before I even arrived at camp I was counting the spots on the roster and the number of people trying to fill them. I've thought a thousand thoughts about what I need to accomplish and how I'm going to make sure I'm in one of those spots. As I write, September 5 fades. Only 25 more days in September. Tomorrow I'll ask the same questions and more. My mind will think of a few additional possibilities and my heart will try to find a home in the pit of my stomach.

Even though I despise the month of September, it feeds the need for the drug (competition) that I've missed all summer long.

- September 14, 1997. *It seems as though this month has six or seven weeks in it. We've been at camp nine days and the end is nowhere in sight. The intrasquad scrimmages have come and gone and we're into the exhibition games, but the mental battle continues within the minds of those on the borderline of making the cut.*

What does it mean that I haven't played in the first two exhibition games and some players have played in both? What does it mean that I'm not on a good line in practice? How long until the next cut? The mind plays tricks on your emotions; you wonder what this means or what that didn't mean. You look for clues that might mean something, and by doing so your mind creates situations and scenarios that most likely don't even exist.

"Control what you can control" is the best advice that you can live by. Playing hard, working hard, and being prepared for your opportunity when it comes is the most you can do. You can tell yourself not to think about it, but your mind has too much time on its hands not to wander and wonder and not to torture the heart with the hope and possibilities of playing in the NHL. The end of the month can't come soon enough and regardless of the outcome, you just want October to start.

- September 16, 1997. *I just got off the phone with Todd Reirden (a teammate from Bowling Green who is at the Edmonton Oilers' camp in a similar situation). We had a chance to exchange stories of our own experiences. Each the same, each with subtle differences. "The coach told me to go on the ice with the second group even though I had just skated with the first group. I wonder if that means I impressed the coaching staff or if I need more work on my skating? Yesterday, I was working out on the bike and the scouts said 'Hello, Todd' as they walked by. What does that mean? At least they know my name. Today they called me in just to talk about how I was playing and to say that I had played better than two of the defensemen who are already under contract. Maybe I'm getting a good look from the scouts and coaching staff."*

Todd and I agreed that neither of us knew what was really going on, that neither of us had any clue when the next bit of factual information would come our way. Frustration had clearly set in and we were both about to go nuts. Just ask my wife.

The only thing that kept me levelheaded today was the ultrasound of the child that lies in my wife's tummy. Maybe the coaching staff would tell me something if I told them the "not knowing" was affecting the well-being of my unborn child.

- September 19, 1997. The L.A. Kings are en route to play the Colorado Avalanche in Las Vegas. It will be my first exhibition game this year. Finally, I get to put my weary mind to rest and focus on playing a game. There are still many jobs up in the air, including mine, but playing in a game allows me to focus on what I'm capable of doing. It's much better than sitting on the sidelines worrying about it.

Control what you can control, that's what I can do. That's what I will do.

Skating onto the ice for warm-ups reminded me of why I put up with the anguish of preseason. The adrenaline was pumping as I skated around the rink. The chance to play in the NHL and live out a dream. You couldn't tell me it was my 80th-something game; it felt like the first. If you could bottle the endorphin coursing through my brain it would be the drug of the century.

I played well. Did my job. I created some offense and was strong defensively. Was it enough? What was their assessment?

"Don't think about it; you controlled what you could. Now let it go."

- September 26, 1997. The Kings have finished five exhibition games and have compiled a solid 4–1 record. The management is left with some difficult decisions heading into the last two exhibition games. Games in which they will want to play what probably will be the starting roster. Three or four forwards still have to be cut. I'll only have to battle my mind for a few more days; the decisions might even be handed down tomorrow. Sleep well.

- September 29, 1997. I was called to the office and told that I was being sent down. I was disappointed but not so much because I was being sent down. It was more because of who was not being sent down and remains on the Kings instead of me. This was not totally unexpected and I find I am not embarrassed. I have been assigned to the Long Beach Ice Dogs and I feel that I will be back soon. I forgive the Kings' management for their obvious mistake in judgment, and trust they're smart enough to see the error of their ways.

- October 16, 1997. Today I woke up in Kansas City as a member of the Long Beach Ice Dogs. Before the day is done I'll be back in L.A.—

a member of the Los Angeles Kings again. Being called back up puts a little spring in my step, but without the nervousness that I felt the first time. I'm excited, yes. But I feel I belong there and I need to prove that sending me down was a mistake. I understand that they're trying to make their team better, but it's my job now to show them that I should be a part of the team. Dan Bylsma is a part of the process of making their team better.

The nervousness isn't there; it won't be there tomorrow morning in practice nor will it be there when I get an opportunity to play in a game. What will be floating around inside of my head will be a sense of urgency to perform the way I know how and in a way that will add something to the L. A. Kings' team.

"Control what you can control. Work hard, be positive, wait for your opportunity, and be ready for it when it comes!"

Thanks Dad, I will be.

Authoring this book has provided me with a unique opportunity to reflect on the turns my life has taken and how one decision has led to the next. It seems that starting with the difficult decision to leave home at the age of fifteen, through my experiences in Canada, college, and the pro ranks, I've had to deal with a lot of setbacks and hard times. My dad thought it was important to relate how I dealt with those repeated situations when the door seemed to be shutting on my dreams.

I thought that was an interesting thing for him to insist on because, as I read about the many turns and detours in my career from *his* viewpoint, I got a sense of his disappointment for me and his concerns about how I was getting along. He was more concerned for me than I was.

How did I react to the cards that life had dealt me? Exactly the way I was taught by my father and mother. Since the day I was born, whether they knew I was watching or not (although I suspect they did), my parents' lives were examples for my siblings and me. I can remember my father, after he had come home from work for dinner and playtime with his children, working late into the morning hours until his work was finished. Sometimes he would come home from the office to take a shower and have dinner and then go back to work.

I remember learning that anything worth doing was worth doing your best. I remember my parents sitting their family down to tell us that my father was quitting his very good job in Chicago after just two years because he felt the company was treating their employees and suppliers dishonestly. I remember being taught that life wasn't fair and how you react to life's unexpected turns more than likely affects your success in the next situation.

I remember how important it was to my parents that each child work hard at doing their very best no matter what the task, be it schoolwork or Little League. I remember that what was important was not the end result of my report card but that I had done my best. I remember that something worthwhile, like an ice rink in the backyard, rarely came about without hard work and determination. I remember that the most important things in life are your family and values, and they shouldn't be taken lightly.

How did I deal with the twists and turns of life? Certainly, I was upset by my experience with my first GM. But going to Canada was the right decision so I gave it another try. Sure, my freshman year at B.G. was disappointing and disheartening. But improving on my year and becoming a contributor wasn't going to happen by hoping a coaching change would occur.

Was giving up after Winnipeg didn't sign me to a contract going to do my dreams of making it to the NHL any good? No, only hard work and proving myself somewhere else would get me a chance to move up the ranks. My parents instilled in me the notion that each decision made leads to the next, and what seems like a big decision today will seem insignificant tomorrow. Because so many things in life are out of our control, it is imperative that we control what can be controlled.

In addition to what I learned through my upbringing, I read a lot. The Bible, Og Mandino's book *The Greatest Miracle in the World* and Robert Schuler's *Tough Times Never Last, Tough People Do* had positive influences on me. Whether ingrained by my parents or acquired from a self-help book, I came to believe that we decide each day what our attitude will be and how hard we're going to work to achieve our goals. Each day we decide whether the rain outside is a good thing or a bad thing, and each day we decide whether a disappointment like getting sent back to the minors is going to make us work hard and be more determined or whether we're going to let it affect us negatively.

I'm not saying that disappointment didn't creep into my head when I didn't get the contract (or whatever) I had hoped for and thought I deserved. Don't think for a second that I didn't worry whether I had made the right decision to go to Canada or that my playing in the NHL was a lost cause. But I never saw the disappointments as stop signs. I saw them as detours, and I merely had to find a different way. To me, that meant working harder or becoming more focused.

Each of us impacts those within the sphere of our influence. With the escalation of salaries for professional athletes and the ever-increasing attention from the media, the sphere of the professional athlete has become very large if not global. Whether we like it or not, athletes are role models. The only question is whether the examples we set are positive or negative. Although some athletes may deny it or may not like or want the eyes of America on their personal lives as well as their feats on the playing field, it is as much a part of being an athlete as collecting those big paychecks and endorsement fees. How professional athletes act on and off the playing field has an effect on an enormous number of individuals, of whom children are the most impressionable. Not to acknowledge that you have an effect or to disclaim that you are a role model doesn't diminish the effect, whether it's positive or negative.

I believe each athlete has a responsibility to have a positive effect on the people who might admire him and his career. Each athlete has a unique opportunity to take the time and effort to make a difference in peoples' lives; whether it is a trip to the children's hospital, a talk at a local school, an act of good sportsmanship, control of a temper tantrum, or control of their social life.

In my first five years in the professional ranks, I was unlucky enough to be designated a rookie three times. I've been through my fair share of situations as a rookie—having to carry the bags, waiting to get on the plane until the veterans got on first, or going last to the buffet table. Although being a rookie in the NHL was the easiest of the three, it also had the greatest impact on my wallet. Let me explain what I mean.

Soon after a team is determined, it is traditional that the team goes out for the "rookie dinner." The dinner is a team event where the players and trainers go to the fanciest, most expensive restaurant the veterans can find. The resulting bill is split among the rookies on the team.

At the beginning of the season we stopped in Ottawa, Ontario, for three days. It was a perfect opportunity for the team to go out and enjoy a really fine team meal, especially if the rookies are paying for it. The dinner was planned for Hy's Restaurant on Halloween. As rookies, we were informed that in addition to picking up the tab, we would have to show up in Halloween costumes.

I shopped at a Goodwill store for my costume, which got rave reviews from the veterans. But that didn't stop them from ordering anything and everything from the menu, as well as wine that only my teammates from Quebec could pronounce. I thought my teammate, Doug Zmolek, was joking when he said he had ordered four lobster tails, but I didn't laugh when the waitress brought out the huge platter.

Unless you're Dutch like me, you can't imagine how hard it was to join in on the feeding frenzy and not just go with a bowl of soup. After all, what's a few more dollars? You might as well be broke as badly bent. When the dishes were cleared, the three of us rookies were left with a fairly good-sized bill. It was definitely a hefty shot to the wallet but I paid gratefully, knowing that there were many guys like me who would kill to be paying for that rookie dinner.

The day the news that Sheldon Kennedy of the Boston Bruins had been sexually abused by his Juniors coach was broadcast over ESPN, the L.A. Kings' locker room became very quiet. I sat by my locker and listened to my teammates react in horror to this terrible tragedy. I wondered how close I came to a similar fate. Thinking about it, I learned that you can sweat and shiver at the same time.

When I'm asked the question, "What was the most embarrassing moment in your life?" there's a singular moment that always comes to mind—although I'd like to forget it. I would have long since repressed this memory except for the reminders I periodically get from the media. It was my fourth game with the Kings. It was also a "Hockey Night in Canada" broadcast, the Saturday night ritual all over Canada and some parts of the U.S. We were playing the Toronto Maple Leafs. The Leafs were beating the Kings pretty handily and Coach Robinson was mixing up the lines trying to find a new fit. It was a chance for me to play with the likes of Jari Kurri and Wayne Gretzky. I experienced one shift on the power play with these two future Hall of Famers and then I got a chance to play a regular shift as well.

A blown hand pass call by the officials caught both teams off guard and it set up Gretzky and me for a two-on-one against a single Leaf defenseman. As we came over the blue line, all I remember thinking was that I needed to open up for a pass from the Great One. It was somewhere between that thought and the next when my skate caught the ice in an unexpected way and I began to lose my edge. Knowing that Gretzky was about to pass the puck for what might have been my first NHL goal I desperately tried to hold on . . . but to no avail. Just as his pass reached the perfect position for my one-time shot, I lost the struggle to stay on my feet. My next memory was sitting on the bench wondering whether I should apologize to the greatest player ever to play the game or just stay clear of him. I chose to steer clear.

Although it took a couple of days to stop replaying that two-on-one over and over in my mind, I knew I wouldn't let one play define my career. What I didn't expect was how many times I would be reminded of that one play. I was sent down after that game so I didn't get a chance to see if the media in L. A. had anything to say about it. Unfortunately, the story made it to the *Grand Rapids Press*. Obviously I would have chosen for the incident not to have happened, much less make the papers, but I wasn't surprised to find some mention about my embarrassing fall. What I *was* surprised about, and still am to this day, is the number of times my career and that fall are mentioned in articles about me. Believe it or not, it's even been mentioned in articles about someone else!

The next year, after I made the team and started to contribute on a regular basis, the media wrote a few stories on me and how I was part of the Kings' new look. Although these articles were meant to cast me in a positive light, the writers couldn't resist making a reference to that two-on-one even though it didn't have anything to do with the current situation. It even surfaced two seasons later in an article in the Ottawa, Ontario, press when it was mentioned in an article about an Ottawa Senator player who was trying to establish himself in the NHL. How the columnist even knew about the two-on-one or why he thought to use it in his article is a mystery to me.

Nonetheless, this is the way I've chosen to think about the fall and answer any questions about it. "How many people get the chance to go on a two-on-one with the greatest player ever to play the game? I wish I would have scored. I wish I would have been able to get a shot off and not fallen down. But . . . I got to play with Wayne Gretzky."

––––––––

After reading my Dad's characterization of what he describes as "the gifts" he believes God has endowed in me, I feel compelled to offer my side of an argument that has been strongly debated between the two of us for several years. His explanation as to why I have always been good in athletics and have been able to find my way to the NHL is that I was blessed with superior athletic genes (although watching him skate and my mother play tennis, you have to wonder where he thinks these superior athletic genes come from). I disagree. I think that all of us, barring a physical handicap or genetic limitation, are born with the same relative physical abilities. The difference in levels of success is the result of how those physical abilities are developed and what you make of them. I do not disagree that I have been given a special gift, but I believe that that gift was not ability. It was my family and my environment.

For me, the whole world as I knew it threw baseballs, kicked footballs, and skated on frozen ponds. I had role models to emulate and these role models taught, coached, coaxed, praised, and affirmed. It was an environment that loved me and in which I thrived. I used that environment to become what I wanted to become. Had I wanted to be a doctor, or, like my brother Jon, a lawyer, this environment would have been an excellent launching pad for those professions as well.

My father's belief, however (although wrong), is not far out of the mainstream of American thought. A recent University of Michigan study indicated that a majority of American teachers believe that good grades are the result of genetic factors, while Asian educators believe good grades are more the result of hard work.

Be aware that both sides of this argument have dangerous edges. If you buy into my Dad's belief that exceptional ability is a genetic gift ordained by the Creator and received by a chosen few, it can be an easy excuse not to work hard to become the best you can be. It's equally as dangerous to believe that anyone can create a Tiger Woods with the right environment. It worked for Earl Woods because he had Tiger, who responded positively to that type of intense training. I believe I drew from my environment to become what I am; my environment didn't create me. It's a subtle but important difference.

My gift, this family into which I was born, remains a significant resource for me, and its members are among my best friends. My dad is a valued advisor who administers my hockey camp with great efficiency and acts as an ex-officio manager. One of my mom's roles is to keep stats on me, which I pooh-poohed until she was able to give my agent some valuable information at contract time. There isn't a GM in the league who can go up against my agent and my mom on an equal footing. Scott, a Financial Advisor at Merrill Lynch, handles my investments. Greg handles my property while I'm gone and lines up very relaxing fishing trips for us when I'm home. Jon handles legal matters for me. My sister Laurie thinks her job is to keep me humble, and she's very good at it. She's also my biggest fan.

Who I am, what I am, and where I am is all due to the love and support of my wife and family. For that I've been a very lucky man.

6

FINAL THOUGHTS

JAY

So your son wants to play in the NHL? Or is it the NFL, the NBA, Major League baseball, or the PGA tour?

Dan's advice for you is to teach your child the words to the song "The Impossible Dream" from *Man of La Mancha*. My advice is for you to be certain that your child does not tilt with windmills.

- *Your responsibility as a parent is to train him for life; the NHL has to come from him.* I reiterate the advice I heard Sparky Anderson give the woman over the radio back in the early seventies. "Your son will make it to the Major Leagues *in spite* of what you do for him, not *because* of what you do for him."

- *Amateur sports are wonderful opportunities for life lessons.* Sports are models of life that an eight-year-old can be taught and understand with great clarity because the cause and effects are immediate. Preparation, practice, coaching, rules, referees, winning, and losing are all there; just like real life.

- *Be able to recognize the characteristics that are necessary for a young athlete to make significant advancement.* They are: the child has to be passionately in love with the sport, and he or she must be willing to work harder at it than very hard (practice, practice, practice). Further, the child must be disciplined; that is, to be both teachable and self-controlled. He or she must have a desire to excel and win. And the child needs time off from the sport to recharge his or her batteries and to gain balance in their lives.

• *Be conservative in assessing your child's potential for the big leagues.* Remember that while your son may be the best player in the twelve-year-old league, elsewhere in the world there are twelve-year-olds who are the best players in a fourteen-year-old league, and there may be some twelve-year-olds who are playing with six-teen-year-olds. It may be more important for your son to have the best grades in his league because it is safe to say that more doctors will come out of the hockey program in your area than NHLers—exponentially. If your child questions this wisdom, have him count the number of medical doctors in your city's phone book and compare that to the number of NHL (or NBA, NFL, MLB, PGA, or combine them all) players who have come from your city.

• *Academics must be of primary importance.* Good grades and test scores are a requirement to get into college regardless of the child's athletic ability, and, a good education will enhance the quality of life during and after sports.

• *The child must learn that the road to the NHL or any professional sport is paved with opportunities disguised as drudgery.* The child should work at each practice, play each game, go through each season and play for each coach as if this were the only opportunity the child will ever get. Prepare for each chance and keep a good attitude, and when the chance comes, go out and do the very best he or she can.

• *Be sure the program in which your child is involved is child-oriented not parent/coach/program-oriented.* That is, make sure the program is about developing kids, not developing the reputation of the coach or the program. How can you tell? If your ten-year-old is developed enough to be a very good player in the eleven-twelve year-old-league but the program insists he play in the nine-ten year-old age bracket because the program wants to have the best nine-ten year-old team possible, that program does not have developing the talent of children as its top priority.

Further, if a program schedules more games than are scheduled in the NHL, that program is not interested in what's good for your child as a person or the well-being of your family. In the NHL, the season is 82 games for adults for whom hockey is a full-time job. In college, the season is 34 games for young adults who need time to get an education. The scheduling of 80 games in one season for a ten-year-old child is the product of an adult mind whose priorities are questionable.

• *Be sure the child's life has balance and proper priorities.* Dare I say piano lessons? Space camp? As to priorities, don't be the parent who would spend $4,500 on one hockey season (gear, ice time, travel, summer camps) but wouldn't consider spending $45 on a math tutor.

• *Avoid any situation where your child is a paper star.* If your child is noticeably the best player in the league, your child is in the wrong league. First, the child will play down to the level required to succeed instead of being forced to improve. Second, the game will revolve around the child and often the child will develop into an excellent individual player but a lousy team player. Third, most coaches will overuse the child, causing self-aggrandizement and burnout. Childhood glories are an expensive trade-off for progress. Also remember that sportswriters are journalists at best; they certainly are not talent evaluators or fortune-tellers.

• *Don't be a drop-off parent.* Attend the child's games to see for yourself that the environment is healthy and the child is progressing. Always have a roll of Life-Savers for those life-saver moments. Remember that if what is important to the child is of no importance to you, very soon what is important to you will be of no consequence to the child.

• *Speak the words "You can do anything you want to" with care.* That advice may be appropriate for task-oriented situations, but it doesn't apply to interpersonal relationships. Sometimes when an athlete can do anything on the playing field, he thinks he can also make a beautiful girl into his idea of a perfect partner. That doesn't work.

• *Because sports administration is a human endeavor, it is not perfect.* Sometimes amateur athletics are played by the golden rule; that is, he who has the gold, rules. And his kid makes the team without regard to his kid's lack of ability or your kid's future superstar status. Sometimes sports are unfair, sometimes they can be destructive. Sometimes life is unfair. That's why parental interaction is very important and the dark side of sports can present opportunities to teach life lessons.

• *Be aware that athletic stardom in any sport is a very narrow road with slippery slopes on both sides.* It can start with the seven-year-old who is better than the other kids and is catered to by his parents and coaches. Then, perhaps, he becomes the high school star that is allowed to "skate by" academically, break training rules and school rules because his play is "necessary" for the team's, and therefore the school's, success.

In college, the "star" becomes a campus hero and gets media attention and even the most inane statement, when seen in print, takes on an apparent importance, when, in fact, newsprint has no known nutritional value. Fueling the problem are preferred classroom scheduling, favoritism in the classroom, young women with questionable motives hanging around the locker room door, and alumni favors. These situations, and the too-common use of alcohol, can make an enticing but potentially deadly mixture that takes significant moral strength to avoid. The realm of professional sports multiplies the hazards of college by adding big money, drugs, cosmetic surgical enhancements, and the chance to be fleeced by experts into the mix.

Should anyone be surprised when big league athletes are discovered to be spendthrifts, alcoholics, drug addicts, men who abuse women, or spoiled brats? No; there are spendthrifts, alcoholics, drug addicts, abusers, and spoiled brats in life as well. Sports are a microcosm of life.

But what has your child gained if he survives the odds, overcomes the disappointments, and perseveres to make it in big league sports, and in the process losses it all because he can't control the things in his life that are his (and all of ours) to manage?

- *Be certain the child's goal of playing in college or the professional ranks is his or her goal and not yours.* This may be Rule #1.

People often remark that I must be very proud of the fact that I have a son in the NHL. I *am* very proud of Dan. But more than the fact that he plays hockey in the NHL, I'm proud of the strength of character he has shown in his dedication, perseverance, and his pursuit of excellence in spite of huge disappointments. I'm more proud that he takes his position of a role model seriously. I'm pleased when he takes the time to touch the life of some youngster in his hockey school or advise some parent who is concerned about his child's progress in the game, or agrees to take precious personal relaxation and training time to play in a charity golf outing or make a public appearance for some worthy cause.

I'm also proud that I am able to say that these same characteristics are apparent in Dan's siblings. They're characteristics that will enable each of them to be successful in their chosen fields, or, as they say, their "real jobs" (vs. Dan's situation where he gets paid for playing games); Scott as a Financial Advisor at Merrill Lynch, Greg as a C.P.A./executive with Harbor Steel, Jon as a trial lawyer with Varnum, Riddering, Schmidt, & Howlett, and Laurie as a Human Resources Administrator for Lear Corporation.

In summary, the things that are the most important to your child's athletic success have nothing to do with the game he or she plays:

- See to the child's value system.
- See to the child's discipline.
- See to the child's academic progress.

So your son would like to play in the NHL? Prepare him for life.

DAN

I'd like share some thoughts about success that perhaps may be new to you. The *Time* magazine in my mailbox today carries a story that Michael

Eisner has exercised the stock options that were granted him when he assumed the chairmanship of the Disney Corporation for $500,000,000. Is that success? Michael Jordan, Wayne Gretzky, Barry Sanders—do they epitomize success? Is success only defined by the stratospheric achievements of the best, the highest paid? Is success an achievement, an end point in the road? Is it to finally drink from one's personal Holy Grail?

Surely, the success experienced by the Eisners and Gretzkys of the world is beyond the grasp of us mere mortals. But *is* the opportunity to become successful only possible for certain people, people with rare genetic qualities that were recessive in the rest of our gene pools? Is it a drink from a Holy Grail that we are incapable of grasping regardless of our efforts?

My experience as a hockey player—a collegiate and professional career that spans nine years and eight teams—is that only a percentage of my teammates (in a highly competitive environment) believe they are not as good today as they can be tomorrow. Only about one in five believe their best is yet ahead, that in the next performance they can acquit themselves better than they did today; that next game, next month or next year, they will be better than before.

Few of my associates consciously think that today's practice is an opportunity to become better than they were yesterday, a chance to become better in their future than they were in their past.

Many players would like to think that next year's statistics will be better than last year's, that there will be an improvement in their situation. But they are quite certain that the determining factors are out of their control; it will be the Fates that decide the future. The coach will or won't play them as much, they will or won't be on the power play, or perhaps they should have been traded to an organization that appreciated them. Their fate is not their fault; they are not responsible.

A few players take it a step further. They are convinced they're in a situation that is detrimental to their well-being; they've been wronged, tomorrow is full of obstacles, and they can't look ahead because they have all they can do to hang on today. No one is surprised, including themselves, when an opportunity is missed, when they don't get a new contract, when they don't get the promotion, or when they get fired.

The University of Michigan study mentioned previously indicates that this attitude may have become endemic in our society. The study found that American students believe the responsibility for good grades lies with the teacher, while Asian-born students believe hard work results in good grades. The notion that we are not immediately responsible for ourselves has grown to a national excuse, if not a disorder. We may be rich or poor, black or white, agile or clumsy, smart or dumb, but we are *not* responsible.

I used to think that the behavior of the guys in the middle of the pack and those at the bottom was indicative of only minor league players. I thought that most guys didn't make it to the NHL because they just weren't committed to getting there. They weren't interested or concerned about making themselves a better person, a better skater, a better player, a better teammate—whatever it took to make it.

Imagine my surprise when I made it to the NHL to find out not everybody at that level worked hard to improve themselves. Included in those who did work hard were superstars who wanted to become just that little bit better. Some were marginal players working hard to hang on to their spot until the next game, the next season, the next contract. Good players, better players, and the best who knew they had to improve to stay in the NHL or to improve their own statistics, and improve the team. They were involved in a continuous process of working on their strengths and improving their weaknesses to be better tomorrow than they were today.

On the other hand, there were more than a few players whose goal appeared to be maintenance rather than improvement. Sure, they wanted better statistics and would have liked to earn even more than they already did, but weren't involved in a process to make themselves better. They weren't concerned with winning or losing. They were more concerned with where they were going out that night or which model Porsche was just right for them. They came to practice and they left. They came to the games and they left. Did we win or lose? Some of them left the impression they didn't care.

There were even some in this group who abused their good fortune. They had made it to the NHL, so it was time to enjoy the fruits of "success." As soon as practice was done or the game was over, it was time to head for the bar and Silicone Valley. They came to practice the latest acceptable time, and left at the earliest possible moment. Optional practices were for others. Their eating, drinking, and sleeping habits were not always conducive to supporting the peak physical exertion demanded at the highest levels of professional sports. It should be no surprise that their careers are often rocky and abbreviated.

I was flabbergasted. I thought that once I reached the highest professional levels of my sport, everyone would be consummate professionals. I had the notion that players would realize that the only way to repay the sport for the opportunity they had was to give it their all. The only dues some players felt compelled to pay were to the Players Union, which was expected to work hard to raise salaries to even higher levels. I thought everyone knew that if you didn't work hard to preserve your talent, you lost it.

When I expressed my incredulity to my father and brothers, they told me it was different verses of the same song in their respective disciplines; that about twenty percent of their colleagues are conscientious, hard-working, and concerned about becoming better. They chided me: "Welcome to the real world, pal. That ringing in your ears? It's the clapper from the bell in the bell-shaped curve. You got graded by it in college and now you're living in it."

The real world. No matter where you go, no matter what level you're at, no matter what sample you take, 20% of the people are sluggers, 60% of the people are getting by, and 20% of the people are slugs. And the roughly 80% who are not successful look at the 20% who are and wonder how they do it.

Am I saying that any of the players in the NHL haven't worked hard to get where they are and don't know what it means to sacrifice? Absolutely not. In a class full of geniuses graded on a curve, 20% of the geniuses will get an "A" and 20% will fail even though the test scores may have ranged from 100% to 90%. Is 90% a bad score? Only in comparison to this class of geniuses and only if you didn't properly prepare and give your best effort for the test.

Further, when the leaders of the team are in the top 20%, everyone is challenged and motivated to become a slugger; to raise their level of expectations, enthusiasm, and effort. When the leaders are not in the top 20%, it is very difficult for a team to have a winning attitude. The bar gets raised every time one moves up the ladder of his or her profession. And at each higher rung, there is a new definition of what it means to be a slugger. Nonetheless, the NHL is not comprised exclusively of sluggers.

To be sure, no one—including me—gives 100% effort (or finds himself in the slugger category) all of the time. There are times when your mind is distracted from the task at hand for any number of reasons, and your legs are like lead despite or because of a lack of your best effort. But it is difficult to understand not *trying* to give your best to your job, your team, your sport, your fans.

I need to clarify two things before I share my ideas on success. One, monetary value is not the only measure of success; two, these ideas carry no guarantees.

There are so many factors outside of your control that success cannot be guaranteed. But what you can guarantee is that when your chance comes, when doors open, when you are presented with an opportunity . . . you will be prepared to make the most of it. You can condition yourself for success. In fact, eventually success will be ordinary and not extraordinary.

The most important thing in achieving success is making that goal the most important thing in your life—making it a #1 priority. Your goal can be becoming a better father, becoming the president of the company or becoming the best penalty killer on your team or in the league. And when your goal becomes the most important thing in your life, you will slowly be tapping into the energy and motivation you need to realize your goal.

If you envision where you are going and set a goal, you can then devise a plan and you will be able to chart your progress. The discipline of setting the goal and planning, in and of itself, sets you on a course. That alone provides you with the motivation and energy necessary for progress.

The second step is to evaluate what you need to change in order to achieve your goal. What are your strengths and weaknesses? What do you need to develop in order to reach your #1 priority? For me, if Dan Bylsma wants to become a better hockey player, he needs to be quicker, a better skater, and handle the puck better. Those are the three weaknesses that he can improve on. His strengths are his intelligence, determination, strength and hard work. How am I going to build on and utilize my strengths and improve my weaknesses? This is the process of honest evaluation. How can I get better?

The third step is setting daily, weekly, monthly goals and a plan to achieve them. What action should I take to better develop my strengths and improve my weaknesses? The steps I take must be done on a regular, if not daily basis. Then, assuming the plan is carried out, I have the satisfaction that I did today what I could to improve myself, of accomplishing a goal. Today, I have been in the business of making myself better.

If you follow that routine, what you will be doing is conditioning yourself for success—and you will be achieving it on a daily basis. Success then is no longer extraordinary; it is ordinary because you attained it yesterday, the week before, and the month before. And soon you will expect yourself to be goal-oriented everyday. You will be in the process each day of making yourself a better person than you were the day before. Your next year will be the best so far because you're in the process of making yourself better. You're not, however, guaranteeing yourself success. What you will be guaranteeing is that you will be prepared when the next opportunity comes. Then you can step through that door and take that promotion. It is a conscious process.

The final goal, more often than not, is not just one step away. What enables us to achieve higher levels is the reevaluation process. This became evident to me when I made it to the NHL. Making it to the NHL was a lifelong dream and goal. So powerful was my dream that I didn't think about what I might do after I achieved the NHL; all my goals were just to get there.

When I finished college and was in the ECHL, the first step in my plan was to make it to the AHL or the IHL During the two and one-half years I played in the AHL and the IHL, the next step was to make it to "the show." In December of my fourth year as a professional, I learned that I was going to play in the NHL. I had breakfast with my mom who was in Milwaukee to see the IHL game I was supposed to be in that night. I called my wife and siblings. I remember getting on the plane to

Los Angeles, having dinner at the Charter House with some of my new teammates, sleeping, waking up and walking into the Great Western Forum (the Kings' home arena). It was the biggest high of my life.

However, as soon as I put on my skates and went on the ice, I realized that I wasn't prepared. I hadn't set my goals for anything higher than just making it. When I got there and experienced it, I thought, "If I would've known what it was going to be like, I would have trained harder." There is no equivalent of a flight simulator for the NHL.

I floundered through two practices and two games. I think I did well for myself, but mentally I was out of place and unprepared. Who was I and what was I doing here? Was this really me on the same bench with Wayne Gretzky and playing against the Toronto Maple Leafs? When I was sent back down to the minors, it was a relief to be back in my apartment in Phoenix with my wife. Los Angeles was scary; Phoenix was safe. The Los Angeles experience was awesome but, mentally, I wasn't ready to play at that level.

When I got to the rink the next morning, my coach in Phoenix called me into his office and congratulated me. "I know you beat the odds of getting into the NHL," he said. "Nobody gave you a chance and you surprised everybody. But I didn't just call you in here to congratulate you and say, 'Great career.' I want to challenge you to take the next step, the step beyond just making it. I want you to evaluate what you saw, evaluate where you are now, and work even harder than you ever have before. I want you to know that *I* believe—and I know *you* believe—that you can stay there and excel there. But you need to dedicate yourself at getting back to the NHL and staying there. It isn't just going to happen, and you know what you need to work on. You need to challenge yourself more than you ever have before."

It took me about a week to digest that conversation, to realize what he was telling me. He was saying that I had achieved the dream that had been against all odds and realistically beyond my grasp. But the success I achieved in getting to "the show" was only a prelude to something better if I was able to refocus and set new goals. Success was not standing in the NHL in a pair of skates. Real success could be achieved if I took the challenge, set the goal, and dedicated the time and the effort to make myself a better player so that if I did get the opportunity to play there again, I would belong there.

Success is not just making it to the NHL; success is a continuum. It happens daily. When you make yourself better on a daily basis, when you set goals and achieve them, you are achieving success. It is not extraordinary. You do not all of a sudden achieve a huge amount of success the day you make it to the NHL or reach whatever goal you have set for yourself. To get there, you have been achieving success all along. You were just making yourself ready for the opportunity and when the opportunity came you were able to capitalize on it. Capitalizing on it means to reevaluate, refocus, and rededicate so that when you get there you can stay there. When you get there, you should be mentally ready to say, "I belong here."

That was my challenge. I had to challenge myself to reevaluate. What did I see in the NHL? How hard were the guys working, what was their skill level, what do I need to do to belong there? And I had to re-dedicate and refocus. This is truly how the successful road (not the road to success) is negotiated.

I often hear successful people being talked about in terms of being fortunate. There is an implication that the things that make them successful are things that aren't available to others. There *must* be a success gene and it is dominant in successful people, recessive in the rest of us. Or perhaps it's luck or being in the right place at the right time. I contend that success more often comes through this process of setting goals, working hard to accomplish the goals and then reevaluating where you are and where you want to go from where you are. In the main it is not luck, it is preparation. It is being ready for the next opportunity when it comes.

Being successful is when opportunity and preparation meet. When you are prepared to walk through the door of success, you are lucky. To those who aren't prepared, the success of others may be perceived as luck. They don't realize that the harder you work, the luckier you become. In hockey, we have a similar corollary, "If you work hard enough, the puck will follow you."

If success is a continuum, then it is not signified by an accomplishment. It is the process of accomplishing noticeable improvement. Success is not something you will have one day, but did not have the day before. Successful means being "full of successes." Thinking of success in that way, it is not something that only Michael Eisner or Wayne Gretzky or someone else with presumed superior genes can attain. I can be successful as a player, as a student, as a coach, as a husband, as a father.

My father used to tell us kids, "To rise above the sea of mediocrity takes only a little effort." All you need to do is move into the percentage of people who work hard and care about improving. If I have successes in lots of little ways, I become full of success—successful. You can, too.

Starting today.

EPILOGUE

<u>DAN</u>

At one time, this book had a nice, neat ending—like a fairy tale—with the young man living out his dreams married to his college sweetheart as they ride off into the sunset. Sure, they had their share of obstacles. But they stuck to their principles, worked hard, and persevered. This was the story of a father passing down his life experiences and knowledge, learned by trials and errors, to a new father-to-be who was preparing to begin the journey of raising his own children.

The son had wondered and worried about becoming a father and the challenges that each new day would bring. Mother- and father-to-be were awestruck by the realization that this new life growing inside their hearts would impact every day of the rest of their lives. But the young man believed that with his wife, their commitment to each other, and with hard work, they would be able to handle any situation that might arise.

Living out the events of this book instilled confidence into the expectant couple. Although the road of parenting was sure to be full of unexpected twists and turns, they felt ready to handle whatever lay ahead. They had spent time talking of the family traditions they would start: from the annual picture to be taken on Thanksgiving Day to the placing of newspapers in front of the fireplace on Christmas Eve so the child could see the footprints Santa made in the soot. Each parent wondered if they would be able to remember their lessons from school when it came time to tutor their little one. They looked forward to sharing their child with grandparents, aunts and uncles, and nieces and nephews, and were sure that this child would know all the love and support a family could provide. Dates for the baptism of the child were being considered;

the parents were eager to bind their child in covenant with God in hopes of nurturing a lifelong relationship.

All was set for the arrival of the little one. January 25 was set as the date to induce labor, a date when the NHL schedule would allow the father to be home for the birthing, and all that was left was the process of crossing off days on the calendar. This book was to end the way it began . . . with a young father drawing his breath through a tight throat looking down at his newborn child and saying words that only the two of them would hear, "You've got a long way to go, little one, and I will be there every step of the way."

Our fairy tale ended on January 13, 1998. The Kings were just finishing practice in San Jose when the trainer called me off the ice. "Your wife is on the phone," he said. I couldn't get off the ice fast enough. I had given Mary Beth the equipment manager's pager number just in case the baby had decided to come early. Now she was calling from the hospital; I was going to become a father!

"Mary Beth?"

"Mr. Bylsma, I'll get your wife," the nurse said. The moment I heard the cracking of my wife's voice and her gasps for air, I knew. All our hopes, all our expectations, all our dreams . . . were gone.

Our love had created a heartbeat, and over the course of thirty-eight weeks that heartbeat had fueled our hopes and dreams for the future. Then, mysteriously, the little heartbeats stopped.

Within the hour I was on a plane back to Los Angeles. Together, we began dealing with the loss of our little baby girl. We had a room full of baby things—a crib, a swing, a bathtub, and many little outfits, all laid out and ready. We had a future full of hopes and dreams. We had hearts full of love. All this was going to go unused.

Worse yet, Mary Beth and I had to go through the normal birthing process. We had to prepare ourselves to meet our little baby girl, and prepare ourselves to say goodbye.

How were we going to cope? How were we going to manage? I felt helpless. I had no way of easing the emotional agony my wife was going through. No way to take away her physical pain of having to go through a stillbirth. No way of knowing just what to say or do in the few moments we'd have with our little girl. No way of dealing with the empty arms and quiet house when we came home from the hospital. No one to turn to that could tell us why. All we had were questions.

I am sharing this horrible experience for two reasons. The most important reason is for Mary Beth and me to preserve the memory of the child we hold in our hearts. We were still the parents of a little baby girl, regardless that she never got to cry. Mary Beth and I were the only two people that met her. Mary Beth and I were the only two people that held her. And we treasure those memories every day. She will always be our first child. And we will hold her in a special place in our hearts forever.

We are also sharing the story of our little angel because it elevates the message of this book to a new level. We've written about raising children to be good people, not to be professional athletes—children that will grow up into honest, hard-working, contributing members of society whether they grow up to be electricians or doctors or hockey players. If we do that, they can dream dreams and deal with the ultimate realities of life as it's dealt to them.

It's one thing to be prepared to deal with the ups and downs of a professional career. Fact is, important as it is to me, dealing with the trials and tribulations of the NHL or getting sent down to Long Beach are not life or death struggles. My father has asserted, and I agree with him, that church, family, school, and sports are important tools we can use to prepare our children for life. Frankly, until January 15, 1998, I didn't fully understand what he meant.

Today, two months after we came home from the hospital without our child, we truly know the love and support family and friends can offer in times of "life." We know how it feels to turn to family with confidence and attempt to cry out the pain of losing our baby. We are grateful to have family and friends who have the courage to hug and talk and visit even though they didn't know what to say, or more perceptively, that there isn't anything to say.

Even though they weren't sure what to say and weren't sure how we would feel about the beautiful children they had at home, they had the courage to be present while we sorted through what had happened. Each of our family members cried along with us and listened to our story even though it might have made them uncomfortable. Pain shared is pain tempered.

Why is it important to have a family that one can grow in? Why is it important to feel the love and support of one another? Because it helps us understand the ultimate realities. The preparation is not for the NHL, it's for life.

The message the minister offered at our wedding was remarkably simple. "Look at each other," he said. "The love the two of you have for each other allows you to catch a glimpse of the face of God and see the love He has for you. God is a mystery, but the love between husband and wife is real. It is the most unique kind of love; use it to feel closer to God."

The love and support of family and friends can also offer a window through which we did see the face of God. Along with our families, we received the love and support of many friends and fans. Our friends from church sent their thoughts and prayers and shared stories of similar misfortunes. Letters and messages surrounded our experience with the loving arms of a church community.

Have I questioned why this happened to our baby girl? Continually. Have we wondered what we had done to deserve such a fate? Daily. Have our psyches begun to scab up? Barely. Do we have good answers? No. But what we do have is the loving arms of a close family, lots of friends and a church community. And from that support we feel the loving arms of God. Do we have answers about life and death? No, but we have experienced the reality of a God that is and a God that loves.

Why is it important to raise your children with a moral compass and in the reality of God? For the realities of life.

Life as I have come to understand it.

Dan Bylsma

Photo Credits

All photographs provided by the Bylsma family
with the following exceptions:

Western Michigan Christian High School Annual, page 93 (left)
Mark McIntyre, page 99
Martin Oravec, page 101
Los Angeles Kings, 103, 104, 105, front cover background, back flap